On Drinking

By Charles Bukowski

Available from Ecco

The Days Run Away Like Wild Horses Over the Hills (1969)
Post Office (1971)
Mockingbird Wish Me Luck (1972)
South of No North (1973)
Burning in Water, Drowning in Flame: Selected Poems 1955–1973 (1974)
Factotum (1975)
Love Is a Dog from Hell (1977)
Women (1978)
You Kissed Lilly (1978)
Play the Piano Drunk Like a Percussion Instrument Until the Fingers Begin to Bleed a Bit (1979)
Shakespeare Never Did This (1979)
Dangling in the Tournefortia (1981)
Ham on Rye (1982)
Bring Me Your Love (1983)
Hot Water Music (1983)
There's No Business (1984)
War All the Time: Poems 1981–1984 (1984)
You Get So Alone at Times That It Just Makes Sense (1986)
The Movie: "Barfly" (1987)
The Roominghouse Madrigals: Early Selected Poems 1946–1966 (1988)
Hollywood (1989)
Septuagenarian Stew: Stories & Poems (1990)
The Last Night of the Earth Poems (1992)

Screams from the Balcony: Selected Letters 1960–1970 (1993)

Pulp (1994)

Living on Luck: Selected Letters 1960s–1970s (Volume 2) (1995)

Betting on the Muse: Poems & Stories (1996)

Bone Palace Ballet: New Poems (1997)

The Captain Is Out to Lunch and the Sailors Have Taken Over the Ship (1998)

Reach for the Sun: Selected Letters 1978–1994 (Volume 3) (1999)

What Matters Most Is How Well You Walk Through the Fire: New Poems (1999)

Open All Night: New Poems (2000)

Night Torn Mad with Footsteps: New Poems (2001)

Beerspit Night and Cursing: The Correspondence of Charles Bukowski & Sheri Martinelli 1960–1967 (2001)

Sifting Through the Madness for the Word, the Line, the Way: New Poems (2003)

The Flash of Lightning Behind the Mountain: New Poems (2004)

Slouching Toward Nirvana (2005)

Come On In! (2006)

The People Look Like Flowers at Last (2007)

The Pleasures of the Damned (2007)

The Continual Condition (2009)

On Writing (2015)

On Cats (2015)

On Love (2016)

Essential Bukowski (2016)

Storm for the Living and the Dead (2017)

On Drinking

CHARLES BUKOWSKI

Edited by Abel Debritto

ecco
An Imprint of HarperCollinsPublishers

 For information, address HarperCollins Publishers, 195 Broadway, New York, NY 10007.

HarperCollins books may be purchased for educational, business, or sales promotional use. For information, please email the Special Markets Department at SPsales@harpercollins.com.

A hardcover edition was first published by 2019 by Ecco, an imprint of HarperCollins Publishers.

FIRST ECCO PAPERBACK EDITION PUBLISHED 2019.

Library of Congress Cataloging-in-Publication Data has been applied for.

ISBN 978-0-06-285794-1

19 20 21 22 23 LSC 10 9 8 7 6 5 4 3 2 1

On Drinking

ants crawl my drunken arms

O ants crawl my drunken arms
and they let Van Gogh sit in a cornfield
and take Life out of the world with a
shotgun,
ants crawl my drunken arms
and they sent Rimbaud
to running guns and looking under rocks
for gold,
O ants crawl my drunken arms,
they put Pound in a nuthouse
and made Crane jump into the sea
in his pajamas,
ants, ants, crawl my drunken arms
as our schoolboys scream for Willie Mays
instead of Bach,
ants crawl my drunken arms
through the drink I reach
for surfboards and sinks, for sunflowers
and the typewriter falls like a heart-attack
from the table
or a dead Sunday bull,
and the ants crawl down my throat
and into my mouth,
and I wash them down with wine
and pull up the shades
and they are on the screen

and on the streets
climbing church towers
and into tire casings
looking for something else
to eat.

[To Jon and Louise Webb]
March 25, 1961

[. . .] What bothers me is when I read about the old Paris groups, or somebody who knew somebody in the old days. They did it then too, the names of old and now. I think Hemingway's writing a book about it now. But in spite of it all, I can't buy it. I can't stand writers or editors or anybody who wants to talk Art. For 3 years I lived in a skid row hotel—before my hemorrhage—and got drunk every night with an x-con, the hotel maid, an Indian, a gal who looked like she wore a wig but didn't, and 3 or 4 drifters. Nobody knew Shostakovich from Shelley Winters and we didn't give a damn. The main thing was sending runners out for liquor when we ran dry. We'd start low on the line with our worst runner and if he failed—you must understand, most of the time there was little or no money—we'd go a little deeper with our next best man. I guess it's bragging but I was top dog. And when the last one staggered through the door, pale and shamed, Bukowski would rise with an invective, don his ragged cloak and stroll with anger and assurance into the night, down to Dick's Liquor Store, and I conned him and forced him and squeezed him until he was dizzy; I would walk in in big anger, not beggary, and ask for what I wanted. Dick never knew whether I had any money or not. Sometimes I fooled him and had money. But most of the time I didn't. But anyhow, he'd slap the bottles in front of me, bag them, and then I'd pick them up with an angry, "Put 'em on my tab!"

And then he'd start the old dance—but, jesus, u owe me such and such already, and you haven't paid anything off in a month and—

And then came the ACT OF ART. I already had the bottles in my hand. It would be nothing to walk out. But I'd slap them down again in front of him, ripping them out of the bag and shoving them toward him, saying, "Here, you *want* these things! I'll take my god damned business somewhere else!"

"No, no," he'd say, "take them. It's all right."

And then he'd get out that sad slip of paper and add onto the total.

"Lemme see that," I'd demand.

And then I'd say, "For Christ's sake! I don't owe you *this* much! What's this item here?"

All this was to make him believe that I was going to pay someday. And then he'd try to con me back: "You're a gentleman. You're not like the others. I trust you."

He finally got sick and sold his business, and when the next one came in I started a new tab . . .

And what happened? At eight o'clock one Sunday morning—EIGHT O'CLOCK!!! gd damn it—there was a knock on the door—and I opened it and there stood an editor. "Ah, I'm so and so, editor of so and so, we got your short story and thought it most unusual; we are going to use it in our Spring number." "Well, come on in," I'd had to say, "but don't stumble over the bottles." And then I sat there while he told me about his wife who thought a lot of him and about his short story that had once been published in *The Atlantic Monthly,* and you know how they talk on. He finally left, and a month or so later the hall phone rang and somebody wanted Bukowski, and this time it was a woman's voice, "Mr. Bukowski, we think you have a very unusual short story and the group was discussing it the other night, but we think it has one weakness and we thought you might want to correct the weakness. It was this: WHY DID THE CENTRAL CHARACTER BEGIN TO DRINK IN THE FIRST PLACE?"

I said, "Forget the whole thing and send the story back," and I hung up.

When I walked back in the Indian looked up over his drink and asked, "Who was it?"

I said, "Nobody," which was the most accurate answer I could give.

[To John William Corrington]
January 14, 1963

[. . .] Born Andernach, Germany, August 16th, 1920. German mother, father with American Army (Pasadena born but of German parentage) of Occupation. There is some evidence that I was born, or at least conceived out of wedlock, but I am not sure. American at age of 2. Some year or so in Washington, D.C., but then on to Los Angeles. The Indian suit thing true. All grotesques true. Between the imbecile savagery of my father, the disinterestedness of my mother, and the sweet hatred of my playmates: "Heinie! Heinie! Heinie!" things were pretty hot all around. They got hotter when I was in my 13th years on, I broke out not with acne, but with these HUGE boils, in my eyes, neck, back, face, and I'd ride the streetcar to the hospital, the charity ward, the old man was not working, and there they'd drill me with the electric needle, which is kind of a wood drill that they stick into people. Stayed out of school a year. Went to L.A. City College a couple of years, journalism. Tuition fee was two dollars but the old man said he couldn't afford to send me anymore. I went to work in the railroad yards, scrubbing the sides of trains with OAKITE. I drank and gambled at night. Had a small room above a bar on Temple Street in the Filipino district, and I gambled at night with the aircraft workers and pimps and etc. My place got to be known and every night it was packed. It was hell getting my sleep. One night I hit big. Big for me. 2 or 3 hundred. I knew they'd be back. Got in a fight, broke a mirror and a couple of chairs but held onto the money and early in the morning caught a bus for New Orleans. Some young gal on there made a play for me, and I let her off at Fort Worth but got as far as Dallas and swung back. Wasted some time there and made N.O. Roomed across from THE GANGPLANK CAFE and began writing. Short stories. Drank the money up, went to work in a comic book house, and soon moved on. Miami Beach. Atlanta. New York. St. Louis. Philly. Frisco. L.A. again. New Orleans again. Then Philly again. Then Frisco again. L.A. again. Around and around. A couple of nights in East Kansas City. Chicago. I stopped writing. I concentrated on drinking. My longest stays were in Philly. I would get up early in the morning and go to a bar there and I would close that bar at night. How I made it, I don't know. Then finally back to L.A. and a wild shack job of seven years drinking. Ended up in same charity hospital. This time not with boils but with my stomach torn open finally with rot gut and agony. 8 pints of blood and 7 pints of glucose transfused in without a stop. My whore came to see me and she was drunk. My old man was with her. The old man gave me a lot of lip and the whore was nasty too, and I told the old man, "Just one more word out of you and I'm going to yank this needle outa my arm, climb off this deathbed and whip your ass!" They left. I came out of there, white and old, in love with sunlight, told never to drink again or death would be mine. I found among changes in myself, that my memory which was once pretty good was now bad. Some brain damage, no doubt, they let me lay there a couple of days in the charity ward when my papers got lost and the papers called for immediate transfusions, and I was out of blood, listening to hammers against my brain. Anyhow, I got on a mail truck and drove it around and delivered letters and drank lightly, experimentally, and then one night I sat down and began writing poetry. What a hell of a thing. Where to send this stuff. Well, I took a shot. There was a magazine called *Harlequin* and I was a fucking clown and it was out in some small town in Texas and maybe they wouldn't know bad stuff when they saw it, so—. There was a gal editor there, and the poor dear went wild. Special edition. Letters followed. The letters got warm. The letters got hot. Next thing I knew the gal editor was in Los Angeles. Next thing I knew we were in Las Vegas for marriage. Next thing I knew I was walking in a small Texas town with the local hicks glaring at me. The gal had money. I didn't know she had money. Or her folks had money. We went back to L.A. and I went back to work, somewhere.

The marriage didn't work. It took 3 years for her to find out that I was not what she had thought I was supposed to be. I was anti-social, coarse, a drunkard, didn't go to church, played horses, cursed when intoxicated, didn't like to go anywhere, shaved carelessly, didn't care for her paintings or her relatives, sometimes stayed in bed 2 or 3 days running etc. etc.

Very little more. I went back to my whore who had once been such a cruel and beautiful woman, and who was no longer beautiful (as such) but who had, magically, become a warm and real person, but she could not stop drinking, she drank more than I, and she died.

There is not much left now. I drink mostly alone and discourage company. People seem to be talking about things that don't count. They are too eager or too vicious or too obvious.

[To John William Corrington]
October 1963

[. . .] Something by Brahms on now, piano. Woman just phoned me, some Brazilian who lives above the Sunset Strip. Maybe I ought to strip her. But I am getting enough and although there's some trouble attached, I feel a sense of normalcy for it all. Have cut the drinking down some, mainly beer. I read in the paper today where the average alcoholic lives to be 51 (which leaves me 8 years), while the av. non-drinker lives to be 70. I think the best years are from 30 to 40; you are definitely out of the childhood thing, know more what you don't want, and usually have the health and strength to go with it. Of course, there's something wrong with all of us & if you pour alcohol over it you get rid of it faster.

[To Jon and Louise Webb]
March 1, 1964

[. . .] I am getting a little drunk, a good wall to hide behind, the coward's flag. I remember once in some city in some cheap room, I believe it was St. Louis, yes, a hotel on the corner and the gas fumes of traffic going to work used to come up and choke my sick lazy lungs, and I'd send her out for beer or wine and she was trying to get me straight, trying to mother me or hang me or figure me, as all women will try to do, and she gave me this old bit: "Drinking is only escapism." Sure, I told her, and thank old red-balled God it is, and when I fuck you, that is escapism too, you may not think it is, to you it might be living, now, let's have a drink.

I wonder where she is now? A big fat black maid with the fattest biggest most loveliest legs in the universe and ideas about "escapism."

beerbottle

a very miraculous thing just happened:
my beerbottle flipped over backwards
and landed on its bottom on the floor,
and I have set it upon the table to foam down,
but the photos were not so lucky today
and there is a small slit along the leather
of my left shoe, but it's all very simple:
we cannot acquire too much: there are laws
we know nothing of, all manner of nudges
set us to burning or freezing; what sets
the blackbird in the cat's mouth
is not for us to say, or why some men
are jailed like pet squirrels
while others nuzzle in enormous breasts
through endless nights—this is the
task and the terror, and we are not
taught why. still, it's lucky the bottle
landed straightside up, and although
I have one of wine and one of whiskey,
this forsooths, somehow, a good night,
and perhaps tomorrow my nose will be longer:
new shoes, less rain, more poems.

brewed and filled by . . .

everything
in my beercan hand
is sad,
the dirt is even
sad
under my fingernails,
and this hand
is like the hand of a
machine
and yet
it is not—
it curves itself completely
(an effort containing magic)
around the
beercan
in a movement the same as
roots
pounding a gladiola
up into the sun of air,
and the beer
goes into me.

FROM

Confessions *of a Man Insane Enough to Live with Beasts*

I was shacked with another one. We were on the 2nd floor of a court and I was working. That's what almost killed me, drinking all night and working all day. I kept throwing a bottle through the same window. I used to take that window down to a glass place at the corner and get it fixed, get a pane of glass put in. Once a week I did this. The man looked at me very strangely but he always took my money which looked all right to him. I'd been drinking heavily, steadily for 15 years, and one morning I woke up and there it was: blood streaming out of my mouth and ass. Black turds. Blood, blood, waterfalls of blood. Blood stinks worse than shit. She called a doctor and the ambulance came after me. The attendants said I was too big to carry down the steps and asked me to walk down. "O.k., men," I said. "Glad to oblige—don't want you to work too hard." Outside I got onto the stretcher; they opened it for me and I climbed on like a wilted flower. One hell of a flower. The neighbors had their heads out the windows, they stood on their steps as I went by. They saw me drunk most of the time. "Look, Mabel," one of them said, "there goes that horrible man!" "God have mercy on his soul!" the answer came.

Good old Mabel. I let go a mouthful of red over the edge of the stretcher and somebody went OOOOOhhhhhhooooh.

Even though I was working I didn't have any money so it was back to the charity ward. The ambulance was packed. They had shelves in the ambulance and everybody was everywhere. "Full house," said the driver, "let's go." It was a bad ride. We swayed, we tilted. I made every effort to hold the blood in as I didn't want to get anybody stinking. "Oh," I heard a Negro woman's voice, "I can't believe this is happening to me, I can't believe it, oh God help me!"

God gets pretty popular in places like that.

They put me in a dark basement and somebody gave me something in a glass of water and that was that. Every now and then I would vomit some blood into the bedpan. There were four or five of us down there. One of the men was drunk—and insane—but he seemed strong. He got off his cot and wandered around, stumbled around, falling across the other men, knocking things over, "Wa wa was, I am wawa the joba, I am juba I am jumma jubba wasta, I am juba." I grabbed the water pitcher to hit him with but he never came near me. He finally fell down in a corner and passed out. I was in the basement all night and until noon the next day. Then they moved me upstairs. The ward was overloaded. They put me in a dark corner. "Ooh, he's gonna die in that dark corner," one of the nurses said. "Yeah," said the other one.

I got up one night and couldn't make it to the can. I heaved blood all over the middle of the floor. I fell down and was too weak to get up. I called for a nurse but the doors to the ward were covered with tin and three to six inches thick and they couldn't hear. A nurse came by about once every two hours to check for corpses. They rolled a lot of dead out at night. I couldn't sleep and used to watch them. Slip a guy off the bed and pull him onto the roller and pull the sheet over his head. Those rollers were well oiled. I hollered, "Nurse!" not knowing especially why. "Shut up!" one of the old men told me, "we want to sleep." I passed out.

When I came to all the lights were on. Two nurses were trying to pick me up. "I told you not to get out of bed," one of them said. I couldn't talk. Drums were in my head. I felt hollowed out. It seemed as if I could hear everything, but I couldn't see, only flares of light, it seemed. But no panic, fear; only a sense of waiting, waiting for anything and not caring.

"You're too big," one of them said, "get in this chair."

They put me in the chair and slid me along the floor. I didn't feel like more than six pounds.

Then they were around me: people. I remember a doctor in a green gown, an operating gown. He seemed angry. He was talking to the head nurse.

"Why hasn't this man had a transfusion? He's down to . . . c.c.'s."

"His papers passed through downstairs while I was upstairs and then they were filed before I saw them. And, besides Doctor, he doesn't have any blood credit."

"I want some blood up here and I want it up here NOW!"

"Who the hell is this guy," I thought, "very odd. Very strange for a doctor."

They started the transfusions—nine pints of blood and eight of glucose.

A nurse tried to feed me roast beef with potatoes and peas and carrots for my first meal. She put the tray before me.

"Hell, I can't eat this," I told her, "this would kill me!"

"Eat it," she said, "it's on your list, it's on your diet."

"Bring me some milk," I said.

"You eat that," she said, and walked away.

I left it there.

Five minutes later she came running into the ward.

"Don't EAT THAT!" she screamed, "you can't HAVE THAT!! There's been a mistake on the list!"

She carried it away and came back with a glass of milk.

As soon as the first bottle of blood emptied into me they sat me up on a roller and took me down to the x-ray room. The doctor told me to stand up. I kept falling over backwards.

"GOD DAMN IT," he screamed, "YOU MADE ME RUIN ANOTHER FILM! NOW STAND THERE AND DON'T FALL DOWN!"

I tried but I couldn't stand up. I fell over backwards.

"Oh shit," he said to the nurse, "take him away."

Easter Sunday the Salvation Army band played right under our window at 5 A.M. They played horrible religious music, played it badly and loudly, and it swamped me, ran through me, almost murdered me. I felt as close to death that morning as I have ever felt. It was an inch away, a hair away. Finally they left for another part of the grounds and I began to climb back toward life. I would say that that morning they probably killed a half dozen captives with their music.

Then my father showed with my whore. She was drunk and I knew he had given her money for drink and deliberately brought her before me drunk in order to make me unhappy. The old man and I were enemies of long standing—everything I believed in he disbelieved and the other way around. She swayed over my bed, red-faced and drunk.

"Why did you bring her like that?" I asked. "Why didn't you wait until another day?"

"I told you she was no good! I always told you she was no good!"

"You got her drunk and then brought her here. Why do you keep knifing me?"

"I told you she was no good, I told you, I *told* you!"

"You son of a bitch, one more word out of you and I'm going to take this needle out of my arm and get up and whip the shit out of you!"

He took her by the arm and they left.

I guess they had phoned them that I was going to die. I was continuing to hemorrhage. That night the priest came.

"Father," I said, "no offense, but please, I'd like to die without any rites, without any words."

I was surprised then because he swayed and rocked in disbelief; it was almost as if I had hit him. I say I was surprised because I thought those boys had more cool than that. But then, they wipe their asses too.

"Father, talk to me," an old man said, "you can talk to me."

The priest went over to the old man and everybody was happy.

Thirteen days from the night I entered I was driving a truck and lifting packages weighing up to 50 pounds. A week later I had my first drink—the one they said would kill me.

I guess someday I'll die in that goddamned charity ward. I just can't seem to get away.

[To Douglas Blazek]
August 25, 1965

[. . .] I wrote Henry Miller the other day to twist 15 bucks from a patron of his who promised same if I mailed Henry 3 more *Crux*. I undersell Stuart and it buys whiskey and some horsebets. like I've got a $70 brake repair bill. the car isn't worth that. anyhow, I was drunk and inferred that Henry shake his patron out of his money tree. the 15 arrived from one source today and the Miller letter from another: partial quote: "I hope you're not drinking yourself to death! and, especially not when you're writing. It's a sure way to kill the source of inspiration. Drink only when you're happy if you can. Never to drown your sorrows. And never drink alone!" of course I don't buy any of this. I don't worry about inspiration. when the writing dies, it dies; fuck it. I drink to keep going another day. and I've found that the best way to drink is to drink ALONE. even with a woman and a kid around, I'm drinking alone. can after can laced with a half pint or pint. and I stretch wall to wall in the light, I feel as if I were filled with meat and oranges and burning suns, and the radio plays and I hit the typer maybe and look down at the torn and ink-stained oilcloth on the kitchen table, a kitchen table in hell; a life, not a season in hell; the stink of everything, myself aging; people turning to warts; everything going, sinking, 2 buttons on shirt missing, belly working out;

days of dull clubbing work ahead—hours running around with their heads chopped-off, and I lift the drink, I pour in the drink, the only thing to do, and Miller asks me to worry about the source of INSPIRATION? I can't look at anything, really look at anything without wanting to tear myself apart. drinking is a temporary form of suicide wherein I am allowed to kill myself and then return to life again. drinking is just a little paste to hold on my arms and my legs and my pecker and my head and the rest. writing is only a sheet of paper; I am something that walks around and looks out of a window. amen.

[To William Wantling]
1965

[. . .] I keep drinking beer and scotch, pouring it down, like into a great emptiness . . . I admit that there is some rock stupidity in me that cannot be reached. I keep drinking, drinking, am as sullen as an old bulldog. always this way: people falling down, off their stools, testing me, and I drink them down, down, down, but really no voice, nothing, I sit I sit like some stupid elf in a pine tree waiting for lightning. when I was 18 I used to win $15 or 20 a week at drinking contests and this kept me alive. until they got wise to me. there was one shit, though, called Stinky who always gave me a hard go. I'd outpsyche him sometimes by drinking an extra in between. I used to run with these thieves and we were always drinking in a vacant room, a room for rent, with a low light . . . we never had a place to stay, but most of these boys were tough, carried guns, but I didn't, still was square, still am. I thought Stinky had me one night and I looked up and he wasn't there and I went in to heave and I didn't even heave, there he was in the bathtub, out out, and I walked out and picked up the money.

Buffalo Bill

whenever the landlord and landlady get
beer-drunk
she comes down here and knocks on my door
and I go down and drink beer with them.
they sing old-time songs and
he keeps drinking until
he falls over backwards in his chair.
then I get up
tilt the chair up
and then he's back at the table again
grabbing at a
beercan.

the conversation always gets around to
Buffalo Bill. they think Buffalo Bill is
very funny. so I always ask,
what's new with Buffalo Bill?

oh, he's in again. they locked him
up. they came and got him.

why?

same thing. only this time it was a
woman from the Jehovah's Witnesses. she
rang his bell and was standing there
talking to him and he showed her his
thing, you know.

she came down and told me about it
and I told her, "why did you bother that
man? why did you ring his bell? he wasn't
doing anything to you!" but no, she had to
go and tell the authorities.

he phoned me from the jail, "well, I did it
again!" "why do you keep doing that?" I
asked him. "I dunno," he said, "I dunno
what makes me do that!" "you shouldn't do
that," I told him. "I know I shouldn't do
that," he told me.

how many times has he done
that?

oh, god, I dunno, 8 or 10 times. he's
always doin' it. he's got a good lawyer, tho,
he's got a damn good
lawyer.

who'd you rent his place to?

oh, we don't rent his place, we always keep his
place for him. we like him. did I tell you about
the night he was drunk and out on the lawn
naked and an airplane went overhead and he
pointed to the lights, all you could see
was the taillights and stuff and he pointed to
the lights and yelled, "I AM GOD,
I PUT THOSE LIGHTS IN THE SKY!"

no, you didn't tell me about
that.

have a beer first and I'll
tell you about it.

I had a beer
first.

Notes of a Dirty Old Man

In Philly, I had the end seat and ran errands for sandwiches, so forth. Jim, the early bartender, would let me in at 5:30 A.M. while he was mopping and I'd have free drinks until the crowd came in at 7:00 A.M. I'd close the bar at 2:00 A.M., which didn't give me much time for sleep. but I wasn't doing much those days—sleeping, eating or anything else. the bar was so run down, old, smelled of urine and death, that when a whore came in to make a catch we felt particularly honored. how I paid the rent for my room or what I was thinking about I am not sure. about this time a short story of mine appeared in *Portfolio* III, along with Henry Miller, Lorca, Sartre, many others. the *Portfolio* sold for $10. a huge thing of separate pages, each printed in different type on colored expensive paper, and drawings mad with exploration. Caresse Crosby the editoress wrote me: "a most unusual and wonderful story. who ARE you?" and I wrote back, "Dear Mrs. Crosby: I don't know who I am. sincerely yours, Charles Bukowski." it was right after that that I quit writing for ten years. but first a night in the rain with *Portfolio*, a very strong wind, the pages flying down the street people running after them, myself standing drunk watching; a big window washer who always ate six eggs for breakfast put a big foot in the center of one of the pages: "here! hey I got one!" "fuck it, let it go, let all the pages go!" I told them, and we went back inside. I had won some sort of bet. that was enough.

about 11 A.M. every morning Jim would tell me I had enough, I was 86'd, to go take a walk. I would go around to the back of the bar and lay down in the alley there. I liked to do this because trucks ran up and down the alley and I felt that anytime might be mine. but my luck ran bad. and every day little negro children would poke sticks in my back, and then I'd hear the mother's voice, "all right now, all right, leave that man alone!" after a while I would get up, go back in and continue drinking. the lime in the alley was the problem. somebody always brushed the lime off of me and made too much of it.

I was sitting there one day when I asked somebody, "how come nobody here ever goes into the bar down the street?" and I was told, "that's a gangster bar. you go in there, you get killed." I finished my drink, got up and walked on down. it was much cleaner in that bar. a lot of big young guys sitting around, kind of sullen. it got very quiet. "I'll take a scotch and water," I told the barkeep.

he pretended not to hear me.

I touched up the volume: "bartender, I said I wanted a scotch and water!"

he waited a long time, then turned, came over with the bottle and set me up. I drained it down.

"now I'll have another one."

I noticed a young lady sitting alone. she looked lonely. she looked good, she looked good and lonely. I had some money. I don't remember where I got the money. I took my drink and went down and sat next to her.

"whatya wanna hear on the juke?" I asked.

"anything. anything you like."

I loaded the thing. I didn't know who I was but I could load a juke box. she looked good. how could she look so good and sit alone?

"bartender! bartender! 2 more drinks! one for the lady and one for myself!"

I could smell death in the air. and now that I smelled it I wasn't so sure whether it smelled any good or not.

"whatch havin', honey? tell the man!"

we'd been drinking about a half an hour when one of the two big guys sitting down at the end of the bar got up, slowly walked down to me. he stood behind, leaned over. she'd gone to the crapper. "listen, buddy, I wanna TELL you something."

"go ahead. my pleasure."

"that's the boss's girl. keep messing and you're going to get yourself killed."

that's what he said: "killed." it was just like a movie. he went back and sat down. she came out of the crapper, sat down next to me.

"bartender," I said, "two more drinks."

I kept loading the juke and talking. then I had to go to the crapper. I went to where it said MEN and I noticed there was a long stairway down. they had the men's crapper down below. how odd. I took the first steps down and then I noticed that I was being followed down by the two big boys who had been at the end of the bar. it was not so much the fear of the thing as it was the strangeness. there was nothing I could do but keep walking on down the steps. I walked up to the urinal, unzipped my fly and started to piss. vaguely drunk, I saw the blackjack coming down. I moved my head just a little and instead of taking it over the ear I caught it straight on the back of my head. the lights went in circles and flashes but it was not too bad. I finished pissing, put it back in and zipped my fly. I turned around. they were standing there waiting for me to drop. "pardon me," I said and then I walked between them and walked up the steps and sat down. I had neglected to wash my hands.

"bartender," I said, "two more drinks."

the blood was coming. I took out my hanky and held it to the back of my head. then the two big boys came up out of the crapper and sat down.

"bartender," I nodded toward them, "two drinks for those gentlemen there."

more juke, more talk, the girl didn't move away from me. I didn't make out most of what she was saying. then I had to piss again. I got up and made for the MEN'S room again. one of the big boys said to the other as I passed, "you can't kill that son of a bitch. he's crazy."

they didn't come down again, but when I came back up I didn't sit by the girl again. I had proved some kind of point and was no longer interested. I drank there the rest of the night and when the bar closed we all went outside and talked and laughed and sang. I had done some drinking with a black-haired kid for the last couple of hours. he came up to me: "listen, we want you in the gang. you've got guts. we need a guy like you."

"thanks, pal. appreciate it but I can't do it. thanks anyhow."

then I walked off. always the old sense of drama.

I hailed a cop car a few blocks down, told them I had been blackjacked and robbed by a couple of sailors. they took me to emergency and I sat under a bright electric light with a doc and a nurse. "now this is gonna hurt," he told me. the needle started working. I couldn't feel a thing. I felt like I had myself and everything under pretty good control. they were putting some kind of bandage on me when I reached out and grabbed the nurse's leg. I squeezed her knee. it felt good to me.

"hey! what the hell's the matter with you?"

"nothing. just joking," I told the doc.

"you want us to run this guy in?" one of the cops asked.

"no, take him home. he's had a rough night."

the cops rode me on in. it was good service. if I had been in L.A. I would have made the tank. when I got to my room I drank a bottle of wine and went to sleep.

I didn't make the 5:30 A.M. opening at the old bar. I sometimes did that. I sometimes stayed in bed all day. about 2 P.M. I heard a couple of women talking outside the window. "I don't know about that new roomer. sometimes he just stays in his room all day with the shades down just listening to his radio. that's all he does."

"I've seen him," said the other, "drunk most of the time, a horrible man."

"I think I'll have to ask him to move," said the first one.

ah, shit, I thought. ah, shit, shit shit shit shit.

I turned Stravinsky off, put on my clothes and walked on down to the bar. I went on in.

"hey, there he is!!!"

"we thought ya got killed!"

"did ya hit that gang bar?"

"yeah."

"tell us about it."

"I'll need a drink first."

"sure, sure."

the scotch and water arrived. I sat down at the end stool. the dirty sunshine around 16th and Fairmount worked its way in. my day had begun.

"the rumors," I began, "about it being a very tough joint are definitely true . . ." then I told them roughly about what I have told you.

the rest of the story is that I couldn't comb my hair for two months, went back to the gang bar once or twice more, was nicely treated and left Philly not much later looking for more trouble or whatever I was looking for. I found trouble, but the rest of what I was looking for, I haven't found that yet. maybe we find it when we die. maybe we don't. you've got your books of philosophy, your priest, your preacher, your scientist, so don't ask me. and stay out of bars with MEN's crapper downstairs.

The Great Zen Wedding

I was in the rear, stuck in with the Rumanian bread, liverwurst, beer, soft drinks; wearing a green necktie, first necktie since the death of my father a decade ago. Now I was to be best man at a Zen wedding, Hollis driving 85 m.p.h., Roy's four-foot beard flowing into my face. It was my '62 Comet, only I couldn't drive—no insurance, two drunk-driving raps, and already getting drunk. Hollis and Roy had lived unmarried for three years, Hollis supporting Roy. I sat in the back and sucked at my beer. Roy was explaining Hollis' family to me one by one. Roy was better with the intellectual shit. Or the tongue. The walls of their place were covered with these many photos of guys bending into the muff and chewing.

Also a snap of Roy reaching climax while jacking off. Roy had done it alone. I mean, tripped the camera. Himself. String. Wire. Some arrangement. Roy claimed he had to jackoff six times in order to get the perfect snap. A whole day's work: there it was: this milky glob: a work of art. Hollis turned off the freeway. It wasn't too far. Some of the rich have driveways a mile long. This one wasn't too bad: a quarter of a mile. We got out. Tropical gardens. Four or five dogs. Big black woolly stupid slobbering-at-the-mouth beasts. We never reached the door—there he was, the rich one, standing on the veranda, looking down, drink in hand. And Roy yelled, "Oh, Harvey, you bastard, so good to see you!"

Harvey smiled the little smile: "Good to see you too, Roy."

One of the big black woollies was gobbling at my left leg. "Call your dog off, Harvey, bastard, good to see you!" I screamed.

"Aristotle, now STOP that!"

Aristotle left off, just in time.

And.

We went up and down the steps with the salami, the Hungarian pickled catfish, the shrimp. Lobstertails. Bagels. Minced dove assholes.

Then we had it all in there. I sat down and grabbed a beer. I was the only one with a necktie. I was also the only one who had bought a wedding gift. I hid it between the wall and the Aristotle-chewed leg.

"Charles Bukowski . . ."

I stood up.

"Oh, Charles Bukowski!"

"Uh huh."

Then:

"This is Marty."

"Hello, Marty."

"And this is Elsie."

"Hello, Elsie."

"Do you *really,*" she asked, "break up furniture and windows, slash your hands, all that, when you're drunk?"

"Uh huh."

"You're a little old for that."

"Now listen, Elsie, don't give me any shit . . ."

"And this is Tina."

"Hello, Tina."

I sat down.

Names! I had been married to my first wife for two-and-one-half years. One night some people came in. I had told my wife: "This is Louie the half-ass and this is Marie, Queen of the Quick Suck, and this is Nick, the half-hobble." Then I had turned to them and said, "This is my wife . . . this is my wife . . . this is . . ." I finally had to look at her and ask: "WHAT THE HELL *IS* YOUR NAME ANYHOW?"

"Barbara."

"This is Barbara," I had told them. . . .

The Zen master hadn't arrived. I sat and sucked at my beer.

Then here came *more* people. On and on up the steps. All Hollis' family. Roy didn't seem to have a family. Poor Roy. Never worked a day in his life. I got another beer.

They kept coming up the steps: ex-cons, sharpies, cripples, dealers in various subterfuges. Family and friends. Dozens of them. No wedding presents. No neckties.

I pushed further back into my corner.

One guy was pretty badly fucked-up. It took him 25 minutes to get up the stairway. He had especially-made crutches, very powerful looking things with round bands for the arms. Special grips here and there. Aluminum and rubber. No wood for that baby. I figured it: watered-down stuff or a bad payoff. He had taken the slugs in the old barber chair with the hot and wet shaving towel over his face. Only they'd missed a few vital spots.

There were others. Somebody taught class at UCLA. Somebody else ran in shit through Chinese fishermen's boats via San Pedro Harbor.

I was introduced to the greatest killers and dealers of the century.

Me, I was between jobs.

Then Harvey walked up.

"Bukowski, care for a bit of scotch and water?"

"Sure, Harvey, sure."

We walked toward the kitchen.

"What's the necktie for?"

"The top of the zipper on my pants is broken. And my shorts are too tight. End of necktie covers stinkhairs just above my cock."

"I think that you are the modern living master of the short story. Nobody touches you."

"Sure, Harvey. Where's the scotch?"

Harvey showed me the bottle of scotch.

"I always drink this kind since you always mention it in your short stories."

"But I've switched brands now, Harv. I found some better stuff."

"What's the name of it?"

"Damned if I can remember."

I found a tall water glass, poured in half scotch, half water.

"For the nerves," I told him. "You know?"

"Sure, Bukowski."

I drank it straight down.

"How about a refill?"

"Sure."

I took the refill and walked to the front room, sat in my corner. Meanwhile there was a new excitement: The Zen master had ARRIVED!

The Zen master had on this very fancy outfit and kept his eyes very narrow. Or maybe that's the way they were.

The Zen master needed tables. Roy ran around looking for tables.

Meanwhile, the Zen master was very calm, very gracious. I downed my drink, went in for a refill. Came back.

A golden-haired kid ran in. About eleven years old.

"Bukowski, I've read some of your stories. I think that you are the greatest writer I have ever read!"

Long blond curls. Glasses. Slim body.

"Okay, baby. You get old enough. We'll get married. Live off of your money. I'm getting tired. You can just parade me around in a kind of glass cage with little airholes in it. I'll let the young boys have you. I'll even watch."

"Bukowski! Just *because* I have long hair, you think I'm a girl! My name is Paul! We were introduced! Don't you *remember*?"

Paul's father, Harvey, was looking at me. I saw his eyes. Then I knew that he had decided that I was not such a good writer after all. Maybe even a bad writer. Well, no man can hide forever.

But the little boy was all right: "That's okay, Bukowski! You are still the greatest writer I have ever read! Daddy has let me read some of your stories . . ."

Then all the lights went out. That's what the kid deserved for his big mouth . . .

But there were candles everywhere. Everybody was finding candles, walking around finding candles and lighting them.

"Shit, it's just a fuse. Replace the fuse," I said.

Somebody said it wasn't the fuse, it was something else, so I gave up and while all the candle-lighting went on I walked into the kitchen for more scotch. Shit, there was Harvey standing there.

"Ya got a beautiful son, Harvey. Your boy, Peter . . ."

"Paul."

"Sorry. The Biblical."

"I understand."

(The rich understand; they just don't do anything about it.)

Harvey uncorked a new fifth. We talked about Kafka. Dos. Turgenev, Gogol. All that dull shit. Then there were candles everywhere. The Zen master wanted to get on with it. Roy had given me the two rings. I felt. They were still there. Everybody was waiting on us. I was waiting for Harvey to drop to the floor from drinking all that scotch. It wasn't any good. He had matched me one drink for two and was still standing. That isn't done too often. We had knocked off half a fifth in the ten minutes of candle-lighting. We went out to the crowd. I dumped the rings on Roy. Roy had communicated, days earlier, to the Zen master that I was a drunk—unreliable—either faint-hearted or vicious—therefore, during the ceremony, don't ask Bukowski for the rings because Bukowski might not be there. Or he might lose the rings, or vomit, or lose Bukowski.

So here it was, finally. The Zen master began playing with his little black book. It didn't look too thick. Around 150 pages, I'd say.

"I ask," said the Zen, "no drinking or smoking during the ceremony."

I drained my drink. I stood to Roy's right. Drinks were being drained all over the place.

Then the Zen master gave a little chickenshit smile.

I knew the Christian wedding ceremonies by the sad rote of experience. And the Zen ceremony actually resembled the Christian, with a small amount of horseshit thrown in. Somewhere along the way, three small sticks were lit. Zen had a whole box of the things—two or three hundred. After the lighting, one stick was placed in the center of a jar of sand. That was the Zen stick. Then Roy was asked to place his burning stick upon one side of the Zen stick, Hollis asked to place hers on the other.

But the sticks weren't quite right. The Zen master, smiling a bit, had to reach forward and adjust the sticks to new depths and elevations.

Then the Zen master dug out a circle of brown beads.

He handed the circle of beads to Roy.

"Now?" asked Roy.

Damn, I thought, Roy always read up on everything else. Why not his own wedding?

Zen reached forward, placed Hollis' right hand within Roy's left. And the beads encircled both hands that way.

"Do you . . ."

"I do . . ."

(This was Zen? I thought.)

"And do you, Hollis . . ."

"I do . . ."

Meanwhile, in the candlelight, there was some asshole taking hundreds of photos of the ceremony. It made me nervous. It could have been the F.B.I.

"*Plick! Plick! Plick!*"

Of course, we were all clean. But it was irritating because it was careless.

Then I noticed the Zen master's ears in the candlelight. The candlelight shone through them as if they were made of the thinnest of toilet paper.

The Zen master had the thinnest ears of any man I had ever seen. *That* was what made him holy! I *had* to have those ears! For my wallet or my tomcat or my memory. Or for under the pillow.

Of course, I knew that it was all the scotch and water and all the beer talking to me, and then, in another way, I didn't know that at all.

I kept staring at the Zen master's ears.

And there were more words.

". . . and you Roy, promise not to take any drugs while in your relationship with Hollis?"

There seemed to be an embarrassing pause. Then, their hands locked together in the brown beads: "I promise," said Roy, "not to . . ."

Soon it was over. Or seemed over. The Zen master stood straight up, smiling just a touch of a smile.

I touched Roy upon a shoulder: "Congratulations."

Then I leaned over. Took hold of Hollis' head, kissed her beautiful lips.

Still everybody sat there. A nation of subnormals.

Nobody moved. The candles glowed like subnormal candles.

I walked over to the Zen master. Shook his hand: "Thank you. You did the ceremony quite well."

He seemed really pleased, which made me feel a little better. But the rest of those gangsters—old Tammany Hall and the Mafia: they were too proud and stupid to shake hands with an Oriental. Only one other kissed Hollis. Only one other shook the hand of the Zen master. It could have been a shotgun wedding. All that *family*! Well, I'd be the last to know or the last to be told.

Now that the wedding was over, it seemed very cold in there. They just sat and stared at each other. I could never comprehend the human race, but *somebody* had to play clown. I ripped off my green necktie, flipped it into the air:

"HEY! YOU COCKSUCKERS! ISN'T ANYBODY HUNGRY?"

I walked over and started grabbing at cheese, pickled-pigs' feet and chicken cunt. A few stiffly warmed up, walked over and grabbed at the food, not knowing what else to do.

I got them to nibbling. Then I left and hit for the scotch and water.

As I was in the kitchen, refilling, I heard the Zen master say, "I must leave now."

"Oooh, don't leave . . ." I heard an old, squeaky and female voice from among the greatest gangland gathering in three years. And even she didn't sound as if she meant it. What was I doing in with these? Or the UCLA prof? No, the UCLA prof belonged there.

There must be a repentance. Or something. Some action to humanize the proceedings.

As soon as I heard the Zen master close the front door, I drained my waterglass full of scotch. Then I ran out through the candlelit room of jabbering bastards, found the door (that was a job, for a moment), and I opened the door, closed it, and there I was . . . about 15 steps behind Mr. Zen. We still had 45 or 50 steps to go to get down to the parking lot.

I gained upon him, lurching, two steps to his one.

I screamed: "Hey, Masta!"

Zen turned. "Yes, old man?"

Old man?

We both stopped and looked at each other on that winding stairway there in the moonlit tropical garden. It seemed like a time for a closer relationship.

Then I told him: "I either want both your motherfucking ears or your motherfucking outfit—that neon-lighted bathrobe you're wearing!"

"Old man, you are crazy!"

"I thought Zen had more moxie than to make unmitigated and offhand statements. You disappoint me, Masta!"

Zen placed his palms together and looked upward.

I told him, "I either want your motherfucking outfit or your motherfucking ears!"

He kept his palms together, while looking upward.

I plunged down the steps, missing a few but still flying forward, which kept me from cracking my head open, and as I fell downward toward him, I tried to swing, but I was all momentum, like something cut loose without direction. Zen caught me and straightened me.

"My son, my son . . ."

We were in close. I swung. Caught a good part of him. I heard him hiss. He stepped one step back. I swung again. Missed. Went way wide left. Fell into some imported plants from hell. I got up. Moved toward him again. And in the moonlight, I saw the front of my own pants—splattered with blood, candle-drippings and puke.

"You've met your master, bastard!" I notified him as I moved toward him. He waited. The years of working as a factotum had not left my muscles entirely lax. I gave him one deeply into the gut, all 230 pounds of my body behind it.

Zen let out a short gasp, once again supplicated the sky, said something in the Oriental, gave me a short karate chop, kindly, and left me wrapped within a series of senseless Mexican cacti and what appeared to be, from my eye, man-eating plants from the inner Brazilian jungles. I relaxed in the moonlight until this purple flower seemed to gather toward my nose and began to delicately pinch out my breathing.

Shit, it took at least 150 years to break into the Harvard Classics. There wasn't any choice: I broke loose from the thing and started crawling up the stairway again. Near the top, I mounted to my feet, opened the door and entered. Nobody noticed me. They were still talking shit. I flopped into my corner. The karate shot had opened a cut over my left eyebrow. I found my handkerchief.

"Shit! I need a drink!" I hollered.

Harvey came up with one. All scotch. I drained it. Why was it that the buzz of human beings talking could be so senseless? I noticed the woman who had been introduced to me as the bride's mother was now showing plenty of leg, and it didn't look bad, all that long nylon with the expensive stiletto heels, plus the little jewel tips down near the toes. It could give an idiot the hots, and I was only half-idiot.

I got up, walked over to the bride's mother, ripped her skirt back to her thighs, kissed her quickly upon her pretty knees and began to kiss my way upward.

The candlelight helped. Everything.

"Hey!" she awakened suddenly, "whatcha think you're *doing?*"

"I'm going to fuck the shit out of you, I am going to fuck you until the shit falls outa your ass! Whatcha thinka that?"

She pushed and I fell backwards upon the rug. Then I was flat upon my back, thrashing, trying to get up.

"Damned Amazon!" I screamed at her.

Finally, three or four minutes later I managed to get to my feet. Somebody laughed. Then, finding my feet flat upon the floor again, I made for the kitchen. Poured a drink, drained it. Then poured a refill and walked out.

There they were: all the goddamned relatives.

"Roy or Hollis?" I asked. "Why don't you open your wedding gift?"

"Sure," said Roy, "why not?"

The gift was wrapped in 45 yards of tinfoil. Roy just kept unrolling the foil. Finally, he got it all undone.

"Happy marriage!" I shouted.

They all saw it. The room was very quiet.

It was a little handcrafted coffin done by the best artisans in Spain. It even had this pinkish-red felt bottom. It was the exact replica of a larger coffin, except perhaps it was done with more love.

Roy gave me his killer's look, ripped off the tag of instructions on how to keep the wood polished, threw it inside the coffin and closed the lid.

It was very quiet. The only gift hadn't gone over. But they soon gathered themselves and began talking shit again.

I became silent. I had really been proud of my little casket. I had looked for hours for a gift. I had almost gone crazy. Then I had seen it on the shelf, all alone. Touched the outsides, turned it upside-down, then looked inside. The price was high but I was paying for the perfect craftsmanship. The wood. The little hinges. All. At the same time, I needed some ant-killer spray. I found some Black Flag in the back of the store. The ants had built a nest under my front door. I took the stuff to the counter. There was a young girl there, I set the stuff in front of her. I pointed to the casket.

"You know what that is?"

"What?"

"That's a casket!"

I opened it up and showed it to her.

"These ants are driving me crazy. Ya know what I'm going to do?"

"What?"

"I'm going to kill *all* those ants and put them in this casket and bury them!"

She laughed. "You've saved my whole day!"

You can't put it past the young ones anymore; they are an entirely superior breed. I paid and got out of there . . .

But now, at the wedding, nobody laughed. A pressure cooker done up with a red ribbon would have left them happy. Or would it have?

Harvey, the rich one, finally, was kindest of all. Maybe because he could afford to be kind? Then I remembered something out of my readings, something from the ancient Chinese:

"Would you rather be rich or an artist?"

"I'd rather be rich, for it seems that the artist is always sitting on the doorsteps of the rich."

I sucked at the fifth and didn't care anymore. Somehow, the next thing I knew, it was over. I was in the back seat of my own car, Hollis driving again, the beard of Roy flowing into my face again. I sucked at my fifth.

"Look, did you guys throw my little casket away? I love you both, you know that! Why did you throw my little casket away?"

"Look, Bukowski! Here's your casket!"

Roy held it up to me, showed it to me.

"Ah, fine!"

"You want it back?"

"No! No! My gift to you! Your only gift! Keep it! Please!"

"All right."

The remainder of the drive was fairly quiet. I lived in a front court near Hollywood (of course). Parking was mean. Then they found a space about a half a block from where I lived. They parked my car, handed me the keys. Then I saw them walk across the street toward their own car. I watched them, turned to walk toward my place, and while still watching them and holding to the remainder of Harvey's fifth, I tripped one shoe into a pantscuff and went down. As I fell backwards, my first instinct was to protect the remainder of that good fifth from smashing against the cement (mother with baby), and as I fell backwards I tried to hit with my shoulders, holding both head and bottle up. I saved the bottle but the head flipped back into the sidewalk, BASH!

They both stood and watched me fall. I was stunned almost into insensibility but managed to scream across the street at them: "Roy! Hollis! Help me to my front door, please I'm hurt!"

They stood a moment, looking at me. Then they got into their car, started the engine, leaned back and neatly drove off.

I was being repaid for something. The casket? Whatever it had been—the use of my car, or me as clown and/or best man . . . my use had been outworn. The human race had always disgusted me. Essentially, what made them disgusting was the family-relationship illness, which included marriage, exchange of power and aid, which like a sore, a leprosy, became then: your next door neighbor, your neighborhood, your district, your city, your county, your state, your nation . . . everybody grabbing each other's assholes in the honeycomb of survival out of a fear-animalistic stupidity.

I got it all there, I understood it as they left me there, pleading.

Five more minutes, I thought. If I can lie here five more minutes without being bothered I'll get up and make it toward my place, get inside. I was the last of the outlaws. Billy the Kid had nothing on me. Five more minutes. Just let me get to my cave. I'll mend. Next time I'm asked to one of their functions, I'll tell them where to put it. Five minutes. That's all I need.

Two women walked by. They turned and looked at me.

"Oh, look at him. What's wrong?"

"He's drunk."

"He's not sick, is he?"

"No, look how he holds to that bottle. Like a little baby."

Oh shit. I screamed up at them:

"I'LL SUCK BOTH YOUR SNATCHES! I'LL SUCK BOTH YOUR SNATCHES DRY, YOU CUNTS!"

"Oooooh!"

They both ran into the high-rise glass apartment. Through the glass door. And I was outside unable to get up, best man to something. All I had to do was make it to my place—30 yards away, as close as three million light years. Thirty yards from a rented front door. Two more minutes and I could get up. Each time I tried it, I got stronger. An old drunk would always make it, given enough time. One minute. One minute more. I could have made it.

Then there they were. Part of the insane family structure of the World. Madmen, really, hardly questioning what made them do what they did. They left their double–red light burning as they parked. Then got out. One had a flashlight.

"Bukowski," said the one with the flashlight, "you just can't seem to keep out of trouble, can you?"

He knew my name from somewhere, other times.

"Look," I said, "I just stumbled. Hit my head. I never lose my sense or my coherence. I'm not dangerous. Why don't you guys help me to my doorway? It's 30 yards away. Just let me fall upon my bed and sleep it off. Don't you think, really, that would be the really decent thing to do?"

"Sir, two ladies reported you as trying to rape them."

"Gentlemen, I would *never* attempt to rape two ladies at the same time."

The one cop kept flashing his stupid flashlight into my face. It gave him a great feeling of superiority.

"Just 30 yards to Freedom! Can't you guys understand that?"

"You're the funniest show in town, Bukowski. Give us a better alibi than that."

"Well, let's see—this thing you see sprawled here on the pavement is the end-product of a wedding, a Zen wedding."

"You mean some woman really tried to *marry* you?"

"Not *me,* you asshole . . ."

The cop with the flashlight brought it down across my nose.

"We ask respect toward officers of the law."

"Sorry. For a moment I forgot."

The blood ran down along my throat and then toward and upon my shirt. I was very tired—of everything.

"Bukowski," asked the one who had just used the flashlight, "why can't you stay out of trouble?"

"Just forget the horseshit," I said, "let's go off to jail."

They put on the cuffs and threw me into the back seat. Same sad old scene.

They drove along slowly, speaking of various possible and insane things—like, about having the front porch widened, or a pool, or an extra room in the back for Granny. And when it came to sports—these were *real* men—the Dodgers still had a chance, even with the two or three other teams right in there with them. Back to the family—if the Dodgers won, they won. If a man landed on the moon, *they* landed on the moon. But let a starving man ask them for a dime—no identification, fuck you, shithead. I mean, when they were in civvies. There hasn't been a starving man yet who ever asked a cop for a dime. Our record is clear.

Then I was pushed through the gristmill. After being 30 yards from my door. After being the only human in a house full of 59 people.

There I was, once again, in this type of long line of the somehow guilty. The young guys didn't know what was coming. They were mixed up with this thing called THE CONSTITUTION and their RIGHTS. The young cops, both in the city tank and the county tank, got their training on the drunks. They had to show they had it. While I was watching they took one guy in an elevator and rode him up and down, up and down, and when he got out, you hardly knew who he was, or what he had been—a black screaming about Human Rights. Then they got a white guy, screaming something about CONSTITUTIONAL

RIGHTS; four or five of them got him, and they rushed him off his feet so fast he couldn't walk, and when they brought him back they leaned him against a wall, and he just stood there trembling, these red welts all over his body, he stood there trembling and shivering.

I got my photo taken all over again. Fingerprinted all over again.

They took me down to the drunk tank, opened that door. After that, it was just a matter of looking for floorspace among the 150 men in the room. One shitpot. Vomit and piss everywhere. I found a spot among my fellow men. I was Charles Bukowski, featured in the literary archives of the University of California at Santa Barbara. Somebody there thought I was a genius. I stretched out on the boards. Heard a young voice. A boy's voice.

"Mista, I'll suck your dick for a quarter!"

They were supposed to take all your change, bills, ident, keys, knives, so forth, plus cigarettes, and then you had the property slip. Which you either lost or sold or had stolen from you. But there was always still money and cigarettes about.

"Sorry, lad," I told him, "they took my last penny."

Four hours later I managed to sleep.

There.

Best man at a Zen wedding, and I'd bet they, the bride and groom, hadn't even fucked that night. But somebody had been.

BUK 68

FROM

Post Office

In bed I had something in front of me but I couldn't do anything with it. I whaled and I whaled and I whaled. Vi was very patient. I kept striving and banging but I'd had too much to drink.

"Sorry, baby," I said. Then I rolled off. And went to sleep.

Then something awakened me. It was Vi. She had stoked me up and was riding topside.

"Go, baby, go!" I told her.

I arched my back now and then. She looked down at me with little greedy eyes. I was being raped by a high yellow enchantress! For a moment, it excited me.

Then I told her. "Shit. Get down, baby. It's been a long hard day. There will be a better time."

She climbed off. The thing went down like an express elevator.

In the morning I heard her walking around. She walked and she walked and she walked.

It was about 10:30 A.M. I was sick. I didn't want to face her. Fifteen more minutes. Then I'd get out.

She shook me. "Listen, I want you to get out of here before my girlfriend shows!"

"So what? I'll screw her too."

"Yeah," she laughed, "yeah."

I got up. Coughed, gagged. Slowly got into my clothes.

"You make me feel like a wash-out," I told her. "I can't be that bad! There must be some good in me."

I finally got dressed. I went to the bathroom and threw some water on my face, combed my hair. If I could only comb that face, I thought, but I can't.

I came out.

"Vi."

"Yes?"

"Don't be too pissed. It wasn't you. It was the booze. It has happened before."

"All right, then, you shouldn't drink so much. No woman likes to come in second to a bottle."

"Why don't you bet me to place then?"

"Oh, stop it!"

"Listen, you need any money, babe?"

I reached into my wallet and took out a twenty. I handed it to her.

"My, you *are* sweet!"

Her hand touched my cheek, she kissed me gently along the side of the mouth.

"Drive carefully now."

"Sure, babe."

I drove carefully all the way to the racetrack.

short non-moon shots to nowhere

you
no faces
no faces
at all
laughing at nothing—
let me tell you
I have drank in skidrow rooms with
imbecile winos
whose cause was better
whose eyes still held some light
whose voices retained some sensibility,
and when the morning came
we were sick but not ill,
poor but not deluded,
and we stretched in our beds and rose
in the late afternoons
like millionaires.

[Lafayette Young]
December 1, 1970

[. . .] nobody understands an alcoholic . . . I started drinking young . . . at 16 and 17, and the next morning I'd always get it—those looks, that hatred. of course, my parents hated me anyhow. But I remember saying to them one morning: "Christ, so I got drunk . . . You people treat me like a murderer . . ." "That's it! That's it!" they said, "what you've done is worse than murder!" they meant it. well, what they meant was that I was socially disgracing them in front of the neighbors, and there might be an excuse for murder, but for drinking . . . never, by god, no! They must have meant it, because when the war came on, they urged me to join the murder . . . it was socially acceptable.

[To Steve Richmond]
March 1, 1971

[. . .] drinking's good for a guy your age, if he needs to stretch out and get the sounds from toe to head. you've got a good place there to do that. it may not be so good in the summer with all the bathers trotting by with their ugly asses but in the winter, it's there. best with drinking, though, to wait until about just before sunset and then start in, slowly, with a bit of classical music going. it's a good writing time—after about an hour of drinking. the cigar. the feeling of peace, even though you know it's temporary, so even in feelings of peace you can say war-like things, let it go. allow yourself to enjoy yourself.

[To John Bennett]
March 22, 1971

[. . .] I'm on the wagon—maybe for a long time—drinking wears and tears me—I'm 50—been drinking 33 years plus—going to take a bit of a rest. too many beatings. I really got down near death, not that *that's* bad, it's being *sick* that's bad, unable to bear up in all the shit of this two-bit existence. I don't know how long I can stay straight but I'm going to give it a bit of a run.

on the wagon

Stevens broke almost as many bottles
as he drank.
he'd crash them into the sink,
wash the whiskey away
pick up the glass and
tell me,
"That's it. I'm through. I'm on
the wagon!"
we'd talk an hour or so
and then he'd say,
"Let's go up to the corner and
get the paper."
we'd get up there and he'd say,
"Wait a minute, I need some
cigarettes."
when we got back
he'd sit and look at me a while
and then bring out the pint,
peel the cellophane, uncap the bottle
and put it to his
lips . . . "Aaaaah!
Care for a nip?"
he finally moved to Cincinnati

and I guess he's
still doing it.
me?
I gave up drinking
yesterday.

drinking

for me
it was or
is
a manner of
dying
with boots on
and gun
smoking and a
symphony music
background.

drinking alone,
I mean.
that's the only
drinking—
drinking alone
being alone
fitting the parts
feeling the parts.

of course
drinking can
kill
you

a cold shower
can
or a painting by
Gaugin
or an old dog
on a hot
day.

I would have to suppose
that one thousand swallows
crossing your marble
overhead
sky
at once
could do
it.

that's why I
drink: waiting for
something like
that.

the angels of Sunday

Sunday night in Los Angeles is the graveyard of the nation,
they are all waiting for Monday morning.
we went into *Shakey's* anyhow.
of course, they didn't have the movies on.
it looked more like a mortuary,
7 people in there.
my friend Dutch was crazy, worked 7 days a week,
and bought a straw hat from one of the waiters
for a buck, they gave me one for
nothing.
we sat there and ate pizza and drank beer.
"Bukowski," said Dutch, "you must be a Chinaman, your eyes
are just little slits, but your nose is too big so you
can't be a Chinaman."
later he put some seats together and stretched out.
I'd been drinking all day so when the guy came in and
sat down at the piano I
got up and danced
throwing my straw up into the air and catching it.
the 7 people watched me.
I blew a kiss to an old grey-haired lady,
but there was nothing I could do for the night
there was nothing I could do for the town.
the night and the town were dead.
there weren't even any police around.
I shook Dutch.

"let's go, I want to get drunk alone."
we walked out, Dutch stealing the beer pitcher.
outside he pissed designs in the parking lot.
then we got into the car and drove away from there,
just two old guys without women
in Los Angeles
the Sunday graveyard of the nation,
and the biggest action I caught all that day and night
was when I burned my fingers
lighting a cigarette outside my door.
then I went in and got drunk,
alone.

FROM

"Charles Bukowski Answers 10 Easy Questions"

Question: What would you say is the best brand of American beer on the market today?

Bukowski: Well, that's a bit difficult. Miller's is the easiest on my system but each new batch of Miller's seems to taste a bit worse. Something is going on there that I don't like. I seem to be gradually going over to Schlitz. And I prefer beer in the bottle. Beer in the can definitely gives off a metallic taste. Cans are for the convenience of storekeepers and breweries. Whenever I see a man drinking out of a can I think, "now there is a damn fool." Also, bottled beer should be in a brown bottle. Miller again errs in putting the stuff into a white bottle. Beer should be protected both from metal and from light.

Of course, if you have the money, it's best to go up the scale and get the more expensive beers, imported or better-made American. Instead of a dollar 35 you have to go a dollar 75 or 2 and quarter and up. The taste is immediately noticeable. And you can drink more with less hangover. Most ordinary American beer is almost poison, especially the stuff that comes out of the spigots at racetracks. This beer actually stinks, I mean, to the nose. If you must buy a beer at the racetrack it is best to let it sit for 5 minutes before drinking it. There is something about the oxygen getting in there that removes some of the stink. The stuff is simply green.

Beer was much better before World War 2. It had *tang* and was filled with sharp little bubbles. It's wash now, strictly flat. You just do the best you can with it.

Beer is better to write with and talk with than whiskey. You can go longer and make more sense. Of course, much depends upon the talker and the writer. But beer is fattening, plenty, and it lessens the sex drive, I mean, both the day you are drinking it and the day after. Heavy drinking and heavy loving seldom go hand in hand after the age of 35. I'd say a good chilled wine is the best way out and it should be drank slowly after a meal, with just perhaps a small glass before eating.

Heavy drinking is a substitute for companionship and it's a substitute for suicide. It's a secondary way of life. I dislike drunks but I do suppose I take a little drink now and then myself. Amen.

drunk
ol' Bukowski
drunk

I hold to the edge of the table
with my belly dangling over my
belt

and I glare at the lampshade
the smoke clearing
over
North Hollywood

the boys put their muskets down
lift high their green-fish beer

as I fall forward off the couch
kiss rug hairs like cunt
hairs

close as I've been in a
long time.

FROM

"Notes on the Life of an Aged Poet"

Most poets read badly. They are either too vain or too stupid. They read too low or too loud. And, of course, most of their poetry is bad. But the audience hardly notices. They are personality gazing. And they laugh at the wrong time and like the wrong poems for the wrong reasons. But bad poets create bad audiences; death brings more death. I had to give most of my early readings while quite intoxicated. Fear was there, of course, fear of reading to them, but the disgust was stronger. At some universities I simply broke out the pint and drank as I read. It seemed to work—the applause was fair enough and I felt little pain from the reading, but it seemed I was not invited back. The only 2nd invites I have received have been at places where I didn't drink at the reading. So much for their measurements of poetry. Now and then, though, a poet does fall upon a magic audience where everything is right. I can't explain how this works. It is very strange—it is as if the poet were the audience and the audience were the poet. It all flows.

Of course, parties after readings can lead to many joys and/or disasters. I remember after one reading that the only room available to me was in the woman's dorm, so we partied there, the profs and a few of the students and after they were gone I still had a bit of whiskey left and a bit of life left and I looked up at the ceiling and drank. Then I realized that, after all, I was THE DIRTY OLD MAN, so I left my room and walked around knocking on doors and demanding entrance. I wasn't very lucky. The girls were nice enough, they laughed. I walked all about knocking on the doors and demanding entrance. Soon I was lost and I couldn't find my room. Panic. Lost in a girls' dorm! It took me what seemed several hours to find my room again. I believe the adventures that come with the readings are what might make them possibly more than survival goals.

Once my ride in from the airport arrived drunk. I wasn't entirely sober. On the way in I read him a dirty poem a lady had written me. It was snowing and the roads were slick. When I reached this particularly erotic line my friend said, "Oh, my god!" and he lost control of the car and we spun and spun and spun, and I told him as we were spinning, "This is it, Andre, we're not going to make it!," and I lifted my bottle and there we tumbled into a ditch, unable to get out. Andre got out and thumbed; I pleaded old age and sat in the car sucking at my bottle. And who picked us up? *Another drunk*. We had 6 packs all over the floor and a 5th of whiskey. That turned out to be some reading.

At another reading, someplace in Michigan, I put down my poems and asked if anybody wanted to arm wrestle. Then while 400 students circled around us I got down on the floor with this student and we began. I beat him and then we all went out and got drunk (after I got my check). I doubt I will ever repeat that performance.

Of course, there are times when you awaken in a young lady's house in bed with her and you realize that you have taken advantage of your poetry or that your poetry has been taken advantage of. I don't believe a poet has any more right to a special young body than a garage mechanic, if as much. This is what spoils the poet: special treatment or his own idea that he is special. Of course, I am special but I don't believe this applies to many of the others . . .

my landlady and my landlord

56, she leans
forward
in the kitchen
2:25 a.
m.
same red
sweater
holes in
elbows

cook him something to
EAT
he says
from the
same red
face

3 years ago
we broke down a tree
fighting
after he caught me
kissing
her.

beer by the
quarts

we drink
    bad beer
        by the
    quarts

she gets up
and
begins to
fry
something

    all night
we sing songs
songs from 1925 a.
d. to
            1939 a.
d.

    we talk about
    short skirts
    Cadillacs the
    Republican Administration
    the depression
    taxes
    horses
    Oklahoma

here
you son of a bitch,
she says.

    drunk
    I lean forward and
    eat.

The Blinds

I moved to Philadelphia for some peace and quiet after New York City. After paying a week's rent in a roominghouse, I walked down the street to look for the nearest bar. Half a block. I walked in and sat down. It was the poor part of town and the bar was fifty years old. You could smell the urine and shit of one-half a century wafting up into the bar from the restrooms.

I ordered a draft. Everybody was talking, screaming up and down the bar. It was unlike Los Angeles bars or San Francisco bars or New York bars or New Orleans bars or the bars of any of the cities I had been in.

It was 4:30 in the afternoon. Two guys were fighting in the center of the room. Everybody ignored them and kept on talking and drinking. The guy to the right of me was named Danny, the guy to the left, Jim. A bottle came looping through the air and just missed Danny's nose. He grinned as it sailed past his cigarette. Then he turned in his seat and said to one of the fighters:

"That was pretty close, you son of a bitch! Come that close again, and you got a real fight on your hands!"

Then he turned away.

Almost every seat was taken. I wondered where they came from, these people, how they made it. Jim was quieter, older, very red-faced. He had a kind of gentle weariness created by thousands of hangovers. It was the bar of the lost and the damned if I had ever seen one.

There were women in there: one dyke who drank as if she didn't enjoy it, a few housewives, fat, merry and a bit stupid, and two or three ladies who had come down from better times and were unattached. As I sat there one girl got up and left with a man. She was back in five minutes.

"Helen! Helen! How do you do it?"

She just laughed.

Another jumped up to try her.

"That must be good. I gotta have some!"

Helen was back in five minutes, sitting over her drink.

"She must have a suction pump for a pussy!"

They all laughed. Helen laughed.

"I gotta try me some of that," said some old guy down at the end of the bar. "I haven't had a hard-on since Teddy Roosevelt took his last hill."

It took Helen ten minutes with that one.

"I want a sandwich," said some guy. "Who's gonna run me an errand for a sandwich?"

"I will," I said. I walked over.

"O.k.," he said, "I want a roast beef on a bun, everything on. You know where Hendrick's is?"

"No."

"One block west and across the street. You can't miss it."

He gave me the money. "Keep the change."

I walked down to Hendrick's. An old guy with a huge belly was behind the counter. "Roast beef on a bun, everything on, to go for some drunk down at Sharkey's. And one beer for this drunk."

"We don't have any draft."

"Bottle's all right."

I drank the beer and took the sandwich back and sat down. A shot of whiskey appeared in front of me. I nodded thanks and drank it down. The juke box played.

A young-looking fellow of about 22 walked down from behind the bar. He wasn't the bartender.

"I need the venetian blinds cleaned around here."

"You sure do. A filthier set of shafts I've never seen."

"The girls clean their pussies with them. Not only that, but I've lost five or six of those slats up there too."

"Probably room for more," I said.

"No doubt. What do you do?"

"Run errands for sandwiches."

"How about the blinds?"

"How much?"

"Five bucks."

"You're on."

Billy Boy (that was his name—he'd married the female owner of the bar, a gal of about 45, and had taken over) brought me two buckets, some suds, some rags and sponges and I took two blinds down, laid them out and began.

"Drinks are free," said Tommy the night bartender, "as long as you're working."

"Shot of whiskey, Tommy."

I walked over to the bar, drank it down, then walked back

to the buckets. It was slow work, the dust had settled into hard grime. I cut my hands several times and when I put them into the soapy water they stung and burned.

"Shot of whiskey, Tommy."

I finally got one set of blinds finished and hung them back up. The patrons of the bar turned and admired my work.

"Jesus. Beautiful."

"It sure helps this place."

"They'll probably raise the price of drinks."

"Shot of whiskey, Tommy."

I drank it at the bar, then turned to get another set of blinds. I took them down, pulled out the slats and laid them on the table. I beat Jim at the pinball machine for a quarter, then I emptied the buckets in the crapper and got fresh water. The juke box played.

The second set went slower. I cut my hands some more. The patrons stopped joking with me. It was simply work. The fun was gone. I doubted that those blinds had been cleaned in ten years. I was a hero, a five-dollar hero, but nobody appreciated me. I won another quarter at pinball, then Billy Boy hollered at me to go back to work. I walked back to the venetian blinds. Helen walked by. I called her over. She was on her way to the women's crapper.

"Helen, I'll have five bucks when I'm finished here. Will that cover?"

"Sure, but you won't be able to get it up after all that drinking."

"Baby, you don't know a real man when you see one."

She laughed. "I'll be here at closing time. If you can still stand up then, you can have it for nothing."

"I'll be standing *tall,* baby!"

Helen laughed again and walked back toward the crapper.

"Shot of whiskey, Tommy."

"Hey, take it easy," said Billy Boy, "or you'll never finish that job tonight."

"Billy, if I don't finish you keep your five."

"It's a deal," said Billy. "All you people heard? Those blinds gotta be finished by closing or no pay."

"We heard, Billy, you cheapass."

"We heard you, Billy."

"One for the road, Tommy."

Tommy gave me another whiskey and I drank it and walked back to the blinds. I began to feel sullen. Everybody else was sitting down drinking and laughing and I was scrubbing the grime off of venetian blinds. But I needed the five. There were three windows. After any number of whiskeys, I had the three sets of blinds up and shining.

I walked up, got another whiskey and said, "O.k., Billy, pay up. I finished the job."

"You're not finished, Hank."

"Why not?"

"There's three more windows in the back room."

"The back room?"

"The back room. The party room."

I walked back there with him. There were three more windows.

"But, Billy, nobody ever comes back here."

"Oh yeah, sometimes we use this room."

"I'll settle for two-fifty, Billy."

"No, you gotta do 'em all or no pay."

I walked back, got my buckets, dumped the water, put in clean water, soap, then took a set of blinds down. There wasn't anybody in the back room. I pulled the blinds apart, put them on a table and looked at them. I went in for another whiskey, brought it back, sat down. My desire was gone.

Jim walked back on his way to the crapper, stopped.

"What's the matter?"

"I can't make it, Jim. I can't go another blind."

"Wait a minute."

When Jim came out of the crapper he went to the bar and brought his beer back. He began cleaning the blinds.

"That's all right, Jim, forget it."

Jim didn't answer. I went to the bar and got another whiskey. When I came back again I noticed one of the old girls taking the blinds down from the other window.

"Careful you don't cut yourself," I said as I sat down.

A few minutes later there were four or five people back there, men and women, and they were all working at the blinds, talking, and laughing. Pretty soon everybody at the bar was back there, even Helen. It didn't seem to take very long. I worked in two more whiskeys. Then it was finished. Billy Boy came back.

"I don't have to pay you," he said.

"Hell, the job's finished."

"But you didn't do it."

"Don't be a cheapass, Billy," somebody said.

"All right. But he had twenty drinks of whiskey."

Billy reached for the five, I had it and we all walked back to the bar.

"All right," I announced, "a drink for everybody! Me too."

I laid down the five.

Tommy went around pouring the drinks. Some nodded to me, some said thanks.

I said, "Thank you, too."

I drank my drink and Tommy picked up the five.

"You owe the bar $3.15," he said.

"Put it on the tab."

"O.k. Name?"

"Chinaski."

"Chinaski. You heard the one about the Polack who . . ."

"I heard it."

The drinks came my way until closing time. On the last drink I looked around. 2 A.M. closing. Helen was gone. Helen had slipped out. Helen had lied. Just like those bitches, I thought, afraid of the long hard ride . . .

I got up and walked back toward my roominghouse. It was a short walk and the moonlight was bright. My footsteps echoed; it almost sounded as if somebody was following me. I looked around. It wasn't true. I was quite alone.

Notes of a Dirty Old Man

This is what killed Dylan Thomas.

I board the plane with my girlfriend, the sound man, the camera man and the producer. The camera is working. The sound man has attached little microphones to my girlfriend and myself. I am on my way to San Francisco to give a poetry reading. I am Henry Chinaski, poet. I am profound, I am magnificent. Balls. Well, yes, I do have magnificent balls.

Channel 15 is thinking of doing a documentary on me. I have on a clean new shirt, and my girlfriend is vibrant, magnificent, in her early thirties. She sculpts, writes, and makes marvelous love. The camera pokes into my face. I pretend it isn't there. The passengers watch, the stewardesses beam, the land is stolen from the Indians, Tom Mix is dead, and I've had a fine breakfast.

But I can't help thinking of the years in lonely rooms when the only people who knocked were the landladies asking for the back rent, or the F.B.I. I lived with rats and mice and wine and my blood crawled the walls in a world I couldn't understand and still can't. Rather than live their life, I starved; I ran inside my own mind and hid. I pulled down all the shades and stared at the ceiling. When I went out it was to a bar where I begged drinks, ran errands, was beaten in alleys by well-fed and secure men, by dull and comfortable men. Well, I won a few fights but only because I was crazy. I went for years without women, I lived on peanut butter and stale bread and boiled potatoes. I was the fool, the dolt, the idiot. I wanted to write but the typer was always in hock. I gave it up and drank . . .

The plane rose and the camera went on. The girlfriend and I talked. The drinks arrived. I had poetry, and a fine woman. Life was picking up. But the traps, Chinaski, watch the traps. You fought a long fight to put the word down the way you wanted. Don't let a little adulation and a movie camera pull you out of position. Remember what Jeffers said—even the strongest men can be trapped, like God when he once walked on earth.

Well, you ain't God, Chinaski, relax and have another drink. Maybe you ought to say something profound for the sound man? No, let him sweat. Let them all sweat. It's their film burning. Check the clouds for size. You're riding with executives from I.B.M., from Texaco, from . . .

You're riding with the enemy.

On the escalator out of the airport a man asks me, "What's all the cameras? What's going on?"

"I'm a poet," I tell him.

"A poet?" he asks, "what's your name?"

"García Lorca," I say . . .

Well, North Beach is different. They're young and they wear jeans and they wait around. I'm old. Where's the young ones of 20 years ago? Where's Joltin' Joe? All that. Well, I was in S.F. 30 years ago and I avoided North Beach. Now I'm walking through it. I see my face on posters all about. Be careful, old man, the suck is on. They want your blood.

My girlfriend and I walk along with Marionetti. Well, here we are walking along with Marionetti. It's nice being with Marionetti, he has very gentle eyes and the young girls stop him on the street and talk to him. Now, I think, I could stay in San Francisco . . . but I know better; it's back to L.A. for me with that machinegun mounted in the front court window. They might have caught God, but Chinaski gets advice from the devil.

Marionetti leaves and there's a beatnick coffeeshop. I have never been in a beatnick coffeeshop. I am in a beatnick coffeeshop. My girl and I get the best—60 cents a cup. Big time. It isn't worth it. The kids sit about sipping at their coffees and waiting for it to happen. It isn't going to happen.

We walk across the street to an Italian cafe. Marionetti is back with the guy from the *S. F. Chronicle* who wrote in his column that I was the best short story writer to come along since Hemingway. I tell him he is wrong; I don't know who is the best since Hemingway but it isn't H.C. I'm too careless. I don't put out enough effort. I'm tired.

The wine comes on. Bad wine. The lady brings in soup, salad, a bowl of raviolis. Another bottle of bad wine. We are too full to eat the main course. The talk is loose. We don't strain to be brilliant. Maybe we can't be. We get out.

I walk behind them up the hill. I walk with my beautiful girlfriend. I begin to vomit. Bad red wine. Salad. Soup. Raviolis. I always vomit before a reading. It's a good sign. The edge is on. The knife is in my gut while I walk up the hill.

They put us in a room, leave us a few bottles of beer. I glance over my poems. I am terrified. I heave in the sink, I heave in the toilet, I heave on the floor. I am ready.

The biggest crowd since Yevtushenko . . . I walk on stage. Hot shit. Hot shit Chinaski. There is a refrigerator full of beer behind me. I reach in and take one. I sit down and begin to read. They've paid $2 a head. Fine people, those. Some are quite hostile from the outset. 1/3 of them hate me, 1/3 of them love me, the other 3rd don't know what the hell. I have some poems that I know will increase the hate. It's good to have hostility, it keeps the head loose.

"Will Laura Day please stand up? Will my love please stand up?"

She does, waving her arms.

I begin to get more interested in the beer than the poetry. I talk between the poems, dry and banal stuff, drab. I am H. Bogart. I am Hemingway. I am hot shit.

"Read the poems, Chinaski!" they scream.

They are right, you know. I try to stay with the poems. But I'm at the refrigerator door much of the time too. It makes the work easier, and they've already paid. I'm told once John Cage came out on stage, ate an apple, walked off, got one thousand dollars. I figured I had a few beers coming.

Well, it was over. They came around. Autographs. They'd come from Oregon, L.A., Washington. Nice pretty little girls too. This is what killed Dylan Thomas.

Back upstairs at the place, drinking beer and talking to Laura and Joe Krysiak. They are beating on the door downstairs. "Chinaski! Chinaski!" Joe goes down to hold them off. I'm a rock star. Finally I go down and let some of them in. I know some of them. Starving poets. Editors of little magazines. Some get through that I don't know. All right, all right—lock the door!

We drink. We drink. We drink. Al Masantic falls down in the bathroom and crashes the top of his head open. A very fine poet, that Al. Well, everybody is talking. It's just another sloppy beerdrunk. Then the editor of a little magazine starts beating on a fag. I don't like it. I try to separate them. A window is broken. I push them down the steps. I push everybody down the steps, except Laura. The party is over. Well, not quite. Laura and I are into it. My love and I are into it. She's got a temper, I've got one to match. It's over nothing, as usual. I tell her to get the hell out. She does.

I wake up hours later and she's standing in the center of the room. I leap out of bed and cuss her. She's on me.

"I'll kill you, you son of a bitch!"

I'm drunk. She's on top of me on the kitchen floor. My face is bleeding. She bites a hole in my arm. I don't want to die. I don't want to die! Passion be damned! I run into the kitchen and pour half a bottle of iodine over my arm. She's throwing my shorts and shirts out of her suitcase, taking her airplane ticket. She's on her way again. We're finished forever again. I go back to bed and listen to her heels going down the hill.

On the plane back the camera is going. Those guys from Channel 15 are going to find out about life. The camera zooms in on the hole in my arm. There is a double shot in my hand.

"Gentlemen," I say, "there is no way to make it with the female. There is absolutely no way."

They all nod in agreement. The sound man nods, the camera man nods, the producer nods. Some of the passengers nod. I drink heavily all the way in, savoring my sorrow, as they say. What can a poet do without pain? He needs it as much as his typewriter.

Of course, I make the airport bar. I would have made it anyhow. The camera follows me into the bar. The guys in the bar look around, lift their drinks and talk about how impossible it is to make it with the female.

My take for the reading is $400.

"What's the camera for?" asks the guy next to me.

"I'm a poet," I tell him.

"A poet?" he asks. "What's your name?"

"Dylan Thomas," I say.

I lift my drink, empty it with one gulp, stare straight ahead. I'm on my way.

another poem about a drunk and then I'll let you go

"man," he said, sitting on the steps,
"your car sure needs a wash and wax job
I can do it for you for 5 bucks.
I got the wax, I got the rags, I got everything
I need."

I gave him the 5 and went upstairs,
when I came down 4 hours later
he was sitting on the steps drunk
and offered me a can of beer.
he said he was going to get the car
the next day.

HE OFFERED ME A BEER.

the next day he got drunk again and
I loaned him a dollar for a bottle of
wine, his name was Mike
a world war II veteran.
his wife worked as a nurse.

the next day I came down and he was sitting
on the steps and he said,
"you know, I been sitting here looking at your car
wondering how I was gonna do it.
I wanna do it real good."

the next day Mike said it looked like rain
and it sure as hell wouldn't make any sense
to wash and wax a car when it was gonna rain.

the next day it looked like rain again.
and the next.
then I didn't see him anymore.
a week later I saw his wife and she said,
"they took Mike to the hospital,
he's all swelled-up, they say it's from
drinking."

"listen," I told her, "he said he was going to wax my
car, I gave him 5 dollars to wax my
car . . ."

BUK
WAS DRINKING WITH HIS WIFE
WHEN THE PHONE RANG.

I was sitting in their kitchen
drinking with his wife
when the phone rang.
she handed the phone to me.
it was Mike, "listen," he said, "come on down and
get me. I can't stand this
place."

when I got there
they wouldn't give him his clothes
so Mike walked to the elevator in his
gown.
we got on and there was a kid driving the
elevator and eating a popsicle.
"nobody's allowed to leave here in a gown,"
he said.

"you drive this thing, kid," I said,
"we'll worry about the gowns."

I stopped at the liquor store for 2 six packs
then went on in. I drank with Mike and his wife until
11 P.M.
then went upstairs . . .

"where's Mike?" I asked his wife 3 days
later.

"Mike died," she said, "he's gone."

"I'm sorry," I said. "I'm very sorry."

it rained for a week after that and I
figured the only way I'd get that 5 back
was to go to bed with his wife
but you know
she moved out a couple of days
later
and an old guy with white hair
moved in there.
he was blind in one eye and
played the French horn.
there was no way I could make it
with him.

I had to wash and wax my own car.

in the name of love and art

I am sitting in front of my typewriter
waiting to get drunk.
my girlfriend who sculpts
wants to do one of me
nude and drunk
bottle in hand
beergut hanging balls hanging cock
dropping along the rug
and rolling
up.
you know,
I am honored.
someday I'll probably be dead
and they'll look at this thing in clay
(she says she's going to do it about
5/8ths the size)
and there I'll sit
holding my beerbottle:
THE DRUNK
Rodin did The Thinker,
now we'll have The DRUNK.

she's coming over with the Polaroid
to take some shots
as soon as I get drunk enough.
I keep telling her,

you know, I live my life just for you,
I oughta write a song about it.

but she doesn't believe me.
but she ought to believe me.
here I sit
drinking this whiskey and beer.
I don't know how many times I'll have to
get drunk in order to perpetuate
her Art. it may take a long time
to finish this sculpture and I very much want it
to be authentic.

I hope this sacrifice of mine will be
long remembered.
I lift another drink and force it
down my throat.
god, how I love that woman!
she'd better get that cock right.

the drunk tank judge

the drunk tank judge is
late like any other
judge and he is
young
well-fed
educated
spoiled and
from a good
family.

we drunks put out our cigarettes and await his
mercy.

those who couldn't make bail are
first. "guilty," they say, they all say,
"guilty."
"7 days." "14 days." "14 days and then you will be
released to the Honor Farm." "4 days." "7 days."
"14 days."

"judge, these guys beat hell out of a man
in there."

"next case, please."

"7 days." "14 days and then you will be released to the Honor Farm."

the drunk tank judge is
young and
overfed. he has
eaten too many meals. he is
fat.

the bail-out drunks are
next. they put us in long lines and
he takes us
quickly. "2 days or 40 dollars." "2 days or 40 dollars." "2 days or 40 dollars." "2 days or 40 dollars."

there are 35 or
40 of us.
the courthouse is on San Fernando Road among the junkyards.

when we go to the bailiff he
tells us,
"your bail will apply."

"what?"

"your bail will apply."

the bail is $50. the court keeps the
ten.

we walk outside and get into our
old automobiles.
most of our automobiles look worse than
the ones in the
junkyards. some of us
don't have any
automobiles. most of us are
Mexicans and poor whites.
the trainyards are across the
street. the sun is up
good.

the judge has very
smooth
delicate
skin. the judge has
fat
jowls.

we walk and we drive away from the
courthouse.

justice.

some people never go crazy

some people never go crazy.
me, sometimes I'll lie down behind the couch
for 3 or 4 days.
they'll find me there.
it's Cherub, they'll say, and
pour wine down my throat
rub my chest
sprinkle me with oils.

then I'll rise with a roar,
rant, rage—curse
them and the universe
as I send them scattering over the
lawn.
I'll feel much better,
sit down to toast and eggs,
hum a little tune,
suddenly become as lovable as a
pink
overfed whale.

some people never go crazy.
what truly horrible lives
they must live.

Notes of a Dirty Old Man

We were both in handcuffs. The cops led us down the stairway between them and sat us in back. My hands were bleeding onto the upholstery, but they didn't seem to care about the upholstery.

The kid's name was Albert and Albert sat there and said, "Jesus, you guys mean you're going to take me and lock me up where I can't get candy and cigarettes and beer, where I can't listen to my record player?"

"Stop your sniveling, will you?" I asked the kid.

I hadn't made the drunk tank for six or eight years. I was due, I was overdue. It was just like driving that long without a traffic ticket—they were just going to get you finally if you drove and they were going to get you finally if you drank. On drunk tank trips vs. traffic tickets the drunk tank led by 18 to seven. Which shows I'm a better driver than I am a drinker.

It was the city jail and Albert and I got separated in the booking. The routine hadn't changed except the doctor asked how my hands got cut.

"A lady locked me out," I said, "so I smashed the door in, a glass door."

The doctor put one band-aid on the worst cut and I was led to the tank.

It was the same. No bunks. Thirty-five men laying on the floor. There were a couple of urinals and a couple of toilets. Ta, ta, ta.

Most of the men were Mexican and most of the Mexicans were between 40 and 68. There were two blacks. No Chinese. I have never seen a Chinese in a drunk tank. Albert was over in the corner talking but nobody was listening, or maybe they were because once in a while somebody would say, "Jesus Christ, shut up, man!"

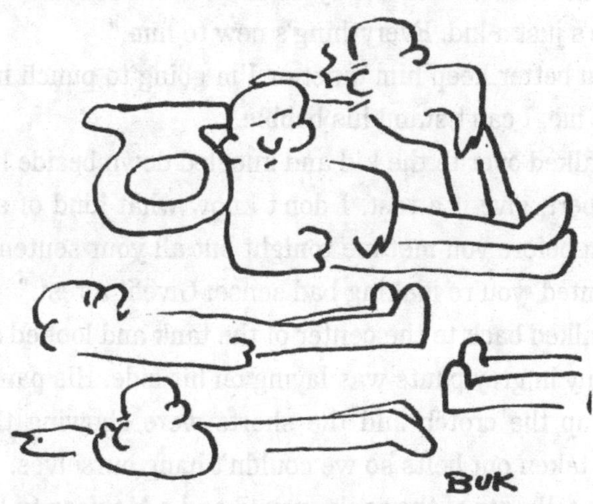

A GUY WAS ASLEEP WITH HIS HEAD AGAINST THE URINAL.

I was the only one standing up. I walked over to one of the urinals. A guy was asleep with his head against the urinal. The guys were all around the urinals and crappers, not using them but sitting crowded around them. I didn't want to step over them so I awakened the guy by the urinal.

"Listen, man, I want to piss and your head is right up against the urinal."

You can never tell when that will mean a fight so I watched him closely. He slid over and I pissed. Then I walked to within three feet of Albert.

"Got a cigarette, kid?"

The kid had a cigarette. He took it out of the pack and threw it at me. It rolled along the floor and I picked it up.

"Anybody got a match?" I asked.

"Here." It was a skid row white. I took the matchbook, struck up a smoke and handed it back.

"What's the matter with your friend?" he asked.

"He's just a kid. Everything's new to him."

"You better keep him quiet or I'm going to punch him out, so help me, I can't stand his babble."

I walked over to the kid and kneeled down beside him.

"Albert, give it a rest. I don't know what kind of shit you were on before you met me tonight but all your sentences are fragmented, you're making bad sense. Give it a rest."

I walked back to the center of the tank and looked around. A big guy in grey pants was laying on his side. His pants were ripped up the crotch and the shorts were showing through. They'd taken our belts so we couldn't hang ourselves.

The cell door of the tank opened and a Mexican in his mid-forties staggered in. He was, as the saying goes, built like a

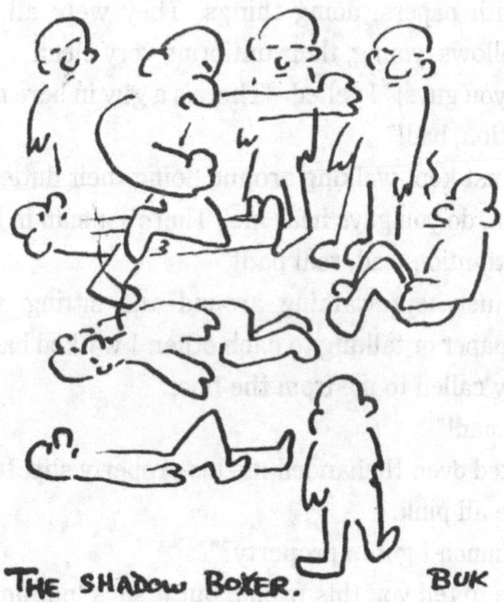

bull. And gored like one. He walked into the tank and did some shadow boxing. He threw some good ones.

Both of his cheeks, up high, near the bone had raw red gashes. His mouth was just a blot of blood. When he opened it all you could see was red. It was a mouth to remember.

He threw a couple more, seemed to miss a hard one, lost balance and fell over backwards. As he fell he arched his back so when he hit the cement the ball of his back took the blow, but he couldn't hold his head back up, it snapped back from the neck, the neck almost acted as a lever and the rear of his head was hurled against the cement. There was the sound, then the head bounced back up, then fell down again. He was still.

I walked over to the tank door. The cops were walking around with papers, doing things. They were all very nice-looking fellows, young, their uniforms very clean.

"Hey, you guys!" I yelled. "There's a guy in here needs medical attention, bad!"

They just kept walking around doing their duties.

"Listen, do you guys hear me? There's a man in here needs medical attention, bad, real bad!"

They just kept walking around and sitting, writing on pieces of paper or talking to each other. I walked back into the cell. A guy called to me from the floor.

"Hey, man!"

I walked over. He handed me his property slip. It was pink. They were all pink.

"How much I got in property?"

"I hate to tell you this friend, but it says 'nothing.'"

I handed his slip back.

"Hey, man, how much I got?" another guy asked me.

I read his and handed it back.

"You're the same; you've got nothing."

"What do you mean, nothing? They took my belt. Isn't my belt something?"

"Not unless you can get a drink for it."

"You're right."

"Doesn't anybody have a cigarette?" I asked.

"Can you roll one?"

"Yeah."

"I got the makings."

I walked over and he handed me the papers and some Bugler. His papers were all stuck together.

"Friend, you've spilled wine all over your papers."

"Good, roll us a couple. Maybe we can get drunk."

I rolled two, we lit up and then I walked over and stood against the tank door and smoked. I looked at them all lying there motionless upon the cement floor.

"Listen, gentlemen, let's talk," I said. "There's no use just laying there. Anybody can lay there. Tell me about it. Let's find something out. Let me hear from you."

There wasn't a sound. I began to walk around.

"Look, we're all waiting for the next drink. We can taste the first one now. To hell with the wine. We want a cold beer, one cold beer to start it out with, to wash the dust out of the throat."

"Yeah," said somebody.

I kept walking around.

"Everybody's talking about liberation now, that's the thing, you know. Do you know that?"

No response. They didn't know that.

"All right, I say let's liberate the roaches and the alcoholics. What's wrong with a roach? Can anybody tell me what's wrong with a roach?"

"Well, they stink and they're ugly," said some guy.

"So's an alcoholic. They sell us the stuff to drink, don't they? Then we drink it and they throw us in jail. I don't understand. Does anybody understand this?"

No response. They didn't understand.

The tank door opened up and a cop stepped in.

"Everybody up. We're moving to another cell."

They got to their feet and walked toward the door. All except the bull. Me and another guy walked over and picked the bull up. We walked him out the door and down the aisle. The cops just watched us. When we got to the next tank we laid the bull down in the center of the floor. The cell door shut.

"As I was saying . . . well, what was I saying? O.k., those of us who have money, we bail out, we get fined. The money we pay is used to pay those who arrested us and kept us confined, and the money is used to enable them to arrest us again. Now, I mean, if you want to call that justice you can call it justice. I call it shit down the throat."

"Alcoholism is a disease," said some guy from flat on his back.

"That's a cliché," I said.

"What's a cliché?"

"Almost everything. O.K., it's a disease but we know they don't know it. They don't throw people with cancer in jail and make them lay on the floor. They don't fine them and beat them. We're the roaches. We need liberation. We should go on parades: 'FREE THE ALCOHOLIC.'"

"Alcoholism is a disease," said the same guy from flat on his back.

"Everything's a disease," I said. "Eating's a disease, sleeping's a disease, fucking's a disease, scratching your ass is a disease, don't you get it?"

"You don't know what a disease is," said somebody.

"A disease is something that's usually infectious, something that's hard to get rid of, something that can kill you. Money is a disease. Bathing is a disease, catching fish is a disease, calendars are a disease, the city of Santa Monica is a disease, bubblegum is a disease."

"How about thumbtacks?"

"Yeah, thumbtacks too."

"What isn't a disease?"

"Now," I said, "now we got something to think about. Now we got something to help us pass the night."

The cell door opened and three cops came in. Two of them walked over and picked up the bull. They walked him out. That broke our conversation somehow. The guys just laid there.

"Come on, come on," I said, "let's keep it going. We'll all have that drink in our hand soon. Some sooner than others. Can't you taste it now? This isn't the end. Think of that first drink."

Some of them laid there thinking about that first drink and some of them laid there thinking about nothing. They were resigned to whatever happened. In about five minutes they brought the bull back in. If he had gotten medical attention it wasn't noticeable. He fell again but this time on his side. Then he was quiet.

"Look, gentlemen, cheer up, for Christ's sake, or for my sake. I know they treat a murderer better than a drunk. A murderer gets a nice cell, a bunk, he gets attention. He's treated like a first-class citizen. He's really done something. All we've done is empty a few bottles. But cheer up, we'll empty some more . . ."

Somebody cheered. I laughed.

"That's better. Look up, look up! God's up there with a couple of six packs of Tuborg. Cold and chilled they are with tiny icy bubbles glistening on the side . . . think of it . . ."

"You're killing me, man . . ."

"You'll be out, we'll be out, some sooner than others. And we won't rush out to an AA meeting and take the 12 great steps back to infancy! Your mother will get you out! Somebody loves you! Now which mother's boy of us will get out of here first? That's something to think about . . ."

"Hey, man . . ."

"Yeah?"

"Come here."

I walked over.

"How much I got?" he asked. He handed me his property slip. I handed it back.

"Brother," I said, "I hate to tell you . . ."

"Yes?"

"It says 'nothing,' a very neatly typed 'nothing.'"

I walked back to the center of the tank.

"Now look, fellows, I'll tell you what I'll do. Everybody take out your property slips and throw them in a pile in the center of the floor. I'll pay a quarter for each pink slip . . . I'll own your souls . . ."

The door opened. It was a cop.

"Bukowski," he announced, "Henry C. Bukowski."

"Be seeing you fellows. It's my mother."

I followed the cop on out. The checkout was fairly efficient. They simply extracted $50 for bail (I'd had a good day at the track) and gave me the rest, plus my belt. I thanked the doctor for his band-aid and followed the cop into the waiting room. I'd made two calls out while being booked. I was told I had a ride. I sat for ten minutes and then a door opened and I was told I could go. My mother was sitting on a bench outside. It was Karen, the 32-year-old woman I lived with. She was trying her damnedest not to be angry but she was. I followed her on out. We got to the car and got in and started off. I looked in the glove compartment for a cigarette.

Even the city hall looks good when you get out of the tank. Everything looks good. The billboards, the stoplights, the parking lots, the bus stop benches.

"Well," said Karen, "now I suppose you'll have something to write about."

"Oh, yeah. And I gave the fellows a good show. The fellows are going to miss me. I'll bet it's like a tomb in there . . ."

Karen didn't appear to be impressed. The sun was about to come up and the lady on the billboard, one strap down on her bathing suit, smiled at me as she advertised a sun tan lotion.

GOD'S UP THERE WITH A COUPLE OF 6 PACKS.

FROM

"Confessions of a Badass Poet"

Question: I figured you'd kick ass, rather than do dishes . . .

Bukowski: No, man, I've had my last fight. I've taken my last beating. I used to get into a fight almost every night. I'd fight bartenders . . . That stuff gets old, gets stale—you get your eyes all cut, and your lips all puffed up, a tooth is loose . . . There's no glory in it. Usually, you're too drunk to fight well, you're starving, you know . . .

This one bartender used to beat me up every night. Tough little fighter. So one day I got mad. I went out, bought a loaf of bread, and a salami. I drank a bottle of port wine. I ate that whole load of bread and the salami—it was the first nourishment I'd had in about a week. And I drank that port wine. I was powerful then! I had food in me!

So we went out to fight this night and I was very strong, and I just thrashed him all over the place. The wine made me crazy in the head. I got him up against the bricks, I hit him half the time and the other half the time I hit the bricks with my hands. They finally pulled me off.

He'd been whipping me every night. So when I walked in, he's down at the end of the bar, he's got his head in his hands, he's saying, "Oh, my head hurts!" and he's got women all around him: "Poor Tommy, here, let me put a wet towel on it!" Hell, when I took my beatings it was, "Hey, Hank, kid!" He got special treatment. So I sat down at the bar and the other bartender said, "I can't serve you, man, after what you did to Tommy."

So I said, "What the hell, he's been whipping me!" And he said, "Well, that doesn't matter."

some picnic

which reminds me
I shacked with Jane for 7 years
she was a drunk
I loved her

my parents hated her
I hated my parents
it made a nice
foursome

one day we went on a picnic
together
up in the hills
and we played cards and drank beer and
ate potato salad and weenies

they talked to her as if she were a living person
at last

everybody laughed
I didn't laugh.

later at my place
over the whiskey
I said to her,
I don't like them
but it's good they treated you
nice.

you damn fool, she said,
don't you see?

see what?

they kept looking at my beer-belly,
they think I'm
pregnant.

oh, I said, well here's to our beautiful
child.

here's to our beautiful child,
she said.

we drank them down.

18,000 to one

it was during a reading at the University of Utah.
the poets had run out of drinks
and while one was reading
5 or 6 of the others of us
got into the car
and drove toward a liquor store
but we were blocked on the road out
by all these cars coming into the football stadium.
we were the only car that wanted to go the other way,
they had us: 18,000 to one.
we blocked one lane and honked.
40 cars honked back.
the cop came up.
"look, officer," I said. "we're poets and we need a drink,"
"turn your car around and go into the stadium," said
the officer.
"look man, we need a drink. we don't want to see the
football game. we don't care who wins. we're poets, we're
reading at The Underwater Poetry Festival
at the University of Utah."
"this traffic can only move one way," said the cop.
"turn your car around and go into the stadium."
"look man, I'm reading in 15 minutes. I'm Charles Bukowski.
you've heard of me, haven't you?"
"turn your car around and go into the stadium."

"shit," said Kamstra who was at the wheel,
and he ran the car up over the curbing
and we drove across the campus lawns
leaving tire marks an inch deep.
I was drunk and I don't know how long we drove
or how we got there
but suddenly we were all standing in a liquor store
and we ordered wine, vodka, beer, scotch, got it and left.
we drove back, sampling our liquids.
we got up there and read the asses right off the
audience.
then we picked up their asses and left.
and UCLA won the football game
something to something.

FROM

"Paying for Horses: An Interview with Charles Bukowski"

Question: At one point in your life, you stopped writing for ten years. Why was that?

Bukowski: It started around 1945. I simply gave up. It wasn't because I thought I was a bad writer. I just thought there was no way of crashing through. I put writing down with a sense of disgust. Drinking and shacking with women became my art form. I didn't crash through there with any feeling of glory, but I got a lot of experience which later I could use—especially in short stories. But I wasn't gathering that experience to write it, because I had put the typewriter down.

I don't know. You start drinking; you meet a woman; she wants another bottle; you get into the drinking thing. Everything else vanishes.

Question: What brought it to an end?

Bukowski: Nearly dying. I ended up in County General Hospital with blood roaring out of my mouth and my ass. I was supposed to die, and I didn't. Took lots of glucose and ten or twelve pints of blood. They pumped it straight into me without stop.

When I walked out of that place, I felt very strange. I felt much calmer than before. I felt—to use a trite term—easygoing. I walked along the sidewalk, and I looked at the sunshine and said, 'Hey, something has happened.' You know, I'd lost a lot of blood. Maybe there was some brain damage. That was my thought, because I had a really different feeling. I had this calm feeling. I talk so slowly now. I wasn't always this way. I was kind of hectic before; I was more going, doing, shooting my mouth off. When I came out of that hospital, I was strangely relaxed.

So I got hold of a typewriter, and I got a job driving a truck. I started drinking huge quantities of beer each night after work and typing out all these poems—I told you that I didn't know what a poem is, but I was writing something in a poem form. I hadn't written many before, two or three, but I sat down and was writing poems all of a sudden. So I was writing again and had all these poems on my hands. I started mailing them out, and it began all over. I was luckier this time, and I think my work had improved. Maybe the editors were readier, had moved into a different area of thinking. Probably all three things helped make it click. I went on writing. [. . .]

Question: Can you write and drink at the same time?

Bukowski: It's hard to write prose when you're drinking, because prose is too much work. It doesn't work for me. It's too unromantic to write prose when you're drinking.

Poetry is something else. You have this feeling in mind that you want to lay down the line that startles. You get a bit dramatic when you're drunk, a bit corny. It feels good. The symphony music is on, and you're smoking a cigar. You lift the beer, and you're going to tap out these five or six or fifteen or thirty great lines. You start drinking and write poems all night. You find them on the floor in the morning. You take out all the bad lines, and you have poems. About sixty percent of the lines are bad; but it seems like the remaining lines, when you drop them together, make a poem.

I don't always write drunk. I write sober, drunk, feeling good, feeling bad. There's no special way for me to be.

Question: Gore Vidal said once that, with only one or two exceptions, all American writers were drunkards. Was he right?

Bukowski: Several people have said that. James Dickey said that the two things that go along with poetry are alcoholism and suicide. I know a lot of writers, and as far as I know they all drink but one. Most of them with any bit of talent are drunkards, now that I think about it. It's true.

Drinking is an emotional thing. It joggles you out of the standardism of everyday life, out of everything being the same. It yanks you out of your body and your mind and throws you up against the wall. I have the feeling that drinking is a form of suicide where you're allowed to return to life and begin all over the next day. It's like killing yourself, and then you're reborn. I guess I've lived about ten or fifteen thousand lives now.

FROM

Factotum

I awakened much later in an upholstered red booth at the back of the bar. I got up and looked around. Everybody was gone. The clock said 3:15. I tried the door, it was locked. I went behind the bar and got myself a bottle of beer, opened it, came back and sat down. Then I went and got myself a cigar and a bag of chips. I finished my beer, got up and found a bottle of vodka, one of scotch and sat down again. I mixed them with water; I smoked cigars, and ate beef jerky, chips, and hard-boiled eggs.

I drank until 5 A.M. I cleaned the bar then, put everything away, went to the door, let myself out. As I did I saw a police car approach. They drove along slowly behind me as I walked.

After a block they pulled up alongside. An officer stuck his head out. "Hey, buddy!"

Their lights were in my face.

"What are you doing?"

"Going home."

"You live around here?"

"Yes."

"Where?"

"2122 Longwood Avenue."

"What were you doing coming out of that bar?"

"I'm the janitor."

"Who owns that bar?"

"A lady named Jewel."

"Get in."

I did.

"Show us where you live."

They drove me home.

"Now, get out and ring the bell."

I walked up the drive. I went up on the porch, rang the bell. There was no answer.

I rang again, several times. Finally the door opened. My mother and father stood there in their pajamas and robes.

"*You're drunk!*" my father screamed.

"Yes."

"Where do you get the money to drink? You don't have any money!"

"I'll get a job."

"*You're drunk! You're drunk! My Son is a Drunk! My Son is a God Damned No-Good Drunk!*"

The hair on my father's head was standing up in crazy tufts. His eyebrows were wild, his face puffed and flushed with sleep.

"You act as if I had murdered somebody."

"*It's just as bad!*"

". . . ooh, shit . . ."

Suddenly I vomited on their Persian *Tree of Life* rug. My mother screamed. My father lunged toward me.

"Do you know what we do to a dog when he shits on the rug?"

"Yes."

He grabbed the back of my neck. He pressed down, forcing me to bend at the waist. He was trying to force me to my knees.

"I'll show you."

"Don't . . ."

My face was almost into it.

"I'll show you what we do to dogs!"

I came up from the floor with the punch. It was a perfect shot. He staggered back all the way across the room and sat down on the couch. I followed him over.

"Get up."

He sat there. I heard my mother. "*You Hit Your Father! You Hit Your Father! You Hit Your Father!*"

She screamed and ripped open one side of my face with her fingernails.

"Get up," I told my father.

"*You Hit Your Father!*"

She scratched my face again. I turned to look at her. She got the other side of my face.

Blood was running down my neck, was soaking my shirt, pants, shoes, the rug. She lowered her hands and stared at me.

"Have you finished?"

She didn't answer. I walked back to the bedroom thinking, I better find myself a job.

• • •

When I got back to Los Angeles I found a cheap hotel just off Hoover Street and stayed in bed and drank. I drank for some time, three or four days. I couldn't get myself to read the want ads. The thought of sitting in front of a man behind a desk and telling him that I wanted a job, that I was qualified for a job, was too much for me. Frankly, I was horrified by life, at what a man had to do simply in order to eat, sleep, and keep himself clothed. So I stayed in bed and drank. When you drank the world was still out there, but for the moment it didn't have you by the throat.

ah, shit

drinking German beer
and trying to come up with
the immortal poem at
5 P.M. in the afternoon.
but, ah, I've told the
students that the thing
to do is not to try.
but when the women aren't
around and the horses aren't
running
what else is there to do?
I've had a couple of
sexual fantasies
had lunch out
mailed three letters
been to the grocery store.
nothing on tv.
the telephone is quiet.
I've run dental floss through
my teeth.
it won't rain and I listen
to the early arrivals from the
8 hour day drive in and park
their cars behind the apartment
house next door.
and I sit drinking German beer

and trying to come up with the
big one.
and I'm not going to make it.
I'm just going to keep drinking
more and more German beer
and rolling smokes
and by 11 P.M. I'll be spread out
on the unmade bed
face up
asleep under the electric
light
still waiting on the immortal
poem
still waiting.

who in the hell is Tom Jones?

I was shacked
with a 24-year-old
girl from New York
City for two weeks,
along about the time
of the garbage strike
out there, and one night
this 34-year-old
woman
arrived and she said,
"I want to see my rival,"
and she did and then
she said, "o, you're a
cute little thing!"
next I knew there was a
whirling of wildcats—such
screaming and scratching,
wounded animal moans,
blood and piss . . .

I was drunk and in my
shorts. I tried to
separate them and fell,
wrenched my knee. then
they were through the
door and down the walk
and out in the street.

squadcars full of cops
arrived. a police helicopter
circled overhead.

I stood in the bathroom
and grinned in the mirror.
it's not often at the
age of 55
that such splendid
action occurs.
it was better than the
Watts riots.

then the 34-year-old
came back in. she had pissed
all over herself and her
clothing was torn and
she was followed by 2 cops
who wanted to know
why.

pulling up my shorts
I tried to explain.

beer

I don't know how many bottles of beer
I have drunk while waiting for things
to get better.
I don't know how much wine and whiskey
and beer
mostly beer
I have drunk after
splits with women—
waiting
for the phone to ring
waiting for the sound of footsteps,
and the phone never rings
until much later
and the footsteps never arrive
until much later
when my stomach is coming up
out of my mouth
they arrive as fresh as spring flowers:
"what the hell have you done to yourself?
it will be 3 days before you can fuck me!"

the female is durable
she lives seven and one half years longer
than a man, and she drinks very little beer
because she knows it's bad for the
figure.

while we are going mad
they are out
dancing and laughing
with horny cowboys.

well, there's beer
sacks and sacks of empty beer bottles
and when you pick them up
the bottles fall through the wet bottom
of the paper sacks
rolling
clanking
spilling grey wet ash
and stale beer,
or the sacks fall over at 4 A.M.
in the morning
making the only sound in your life.

beer
rivers and seas of beer
beer beer beer
the radio singing love
songs
as the phone remains silent
and the walls stand
straight up and down
the beer is all there is.

shit time

half drunk
I left her place
her warm blankets
and I was hungover
didn't even know what town
it was.
I walked along and
I couldn't find my car.
but I knew it was somewhere.
and then I was lost
too.
I walked around. it was a
Wednesday morning and I could
see the ocean to the south.
but all that drinking:
the shit was about to pour
out of me.
I walked towards the
sea.
I saw a brown brick
structure at the edge
of the sea.
I walked in. there was an
old guy groaning on one of

the pots.
"hi, buddy," he said.
"hi," I said.
"it's hell out there,
isn't it?" the old guy
asked.
"it is," I answered.
"need a drink?"
"never before noon."
"what time you got?"
"11:58."
"we got two minutes."
I wiped, flushed, pulled up my
pants and walked over.
the old man was still on his pot,
groaning.
he pointed to a bottle of wine
at his feet
it was almost done
and I picked it up and took about
half what remained.
I handed him a very old and wrinkled
dollar
then walked outside on the lawn
and puked it up.
I looked at the ocean and the
ocean looked good, full of blues and
greens and sharks.
I walked back out of there
and down the street

determined to find my automobile.
it took me one hour and 15 minutes
and when I found it
I got in and drove off
pretending that I knew just as much
as the next
man.

FROM

"Buk: The Pock-Marked Poetry of Charles Bukowski. Notes of a Dirty Old Mankind"

Bukowski: I've been drinking beer most of the day, but don't worry, kid, I'm not gonna stick my fist through the window or bust up any furniture. I'm a pretty benign beer drinker . . . most of the time. It's the whiskey that gets me in trouble. When I'm drinking it around people, I tend to get silly or pugnacious or wild, which can cause problems. So when I drink it these days, I try to drink it alone. That's the sign of a good whiskey drinker anyway—drinking it by yourself shows a proper reverence for it. The stuff even makes the lampshades look different. Norman Mailer has uttered a lot of shit, but he said one thing I thought was great. He said, "Most Americans get their spiritual inspiration when they're intoxicated, and I'm one of those Americans." A statement I'll back up 100%, *The Naked and the Dead* be damned. Only thing is, a man has to be careful how he mixes his alcohol and his sex. The best thing for a wise man is to have his sex before he gets drunk 'cause alcohol takes away from that old stem down there. I've been fairly successful at that so far.

FROM

"Charles Bukowski. Dialog with a Dirty Old Man"

Question: Would you characterize yourself as being an alcoholic?

Bukowski: Hell, yes.

Question: Why do you drink so much?

Bukowski: Basically, I'm a very bashful person—I've got a lot of self-doubt—but at the same time I have a tremendous ego. Something about alcohol erases the self-doubt and allows the ego to come out. I've had a lot of experiences and, I think, one thing about drinking is, it leads you to avenues you would never find if you didn't drink. You take chances, you take gambles.

One time I was coming from the racetrack. I had had a fight with my girlfriend, and when I fight with a woman I get very upset. I had won about $180 that night, and I was drunker than shit. So I'm driving along, and when I stopped for a moment at a stop sign, four black guys in a car behind me hit my bumper and pushed me a little. When a guy's had a fight with a woman you don't want to mess with him, you know. He's a killer. So I let them go around me. They went up to the next stop sign, and I went up and pushed their bumper—hard. At the next stop sign, I pushed their bumper *harder*, and all of a sudden they started trying to get away—four black guys, big—and I'm following them. We're turning corners, we're screeching. Here's one white old man chasing four black young cats in a car. "I'll kill you," I yelled. We're skidding, just like a movie, and I feel like I can do it, you know. When you feel like you can do it, who knows? We're screeching, and suddenly they pull up to a curb and I park behind them. Finally I'm going to get to beat the shit out of all four of these guys. They could have been white; they just happened to be black, you know. I'm antiblack, true. I'm antiyellow, antianything. Anyway, I opened my car door and got out. I'm in a big peacoat that makes me look bigger than I am. I came stalking up, and I'm ready to grab them . . . and the minute I start moving toward their car, vroom, they took off. I jumped back in my car, but I lost them.

Question: Did you say you're antiblack?

Bukowski: Yeah. I'm antiblack, also antiyellow.

Question: Are you antiwhite?

Bukowski: Yes, I am.

Question: What is it about blacks that you dislike?

Bukowski: They drive four in a car. And they hit my bumper. Anyway, drinking leads you into avenues where courage can't take you.

Question: Or wisdom refuses to.

Bukowski: Things happen. Drinking makes things happen.

smashed

look, I say, look at *that* house!
wouldn't that be a wonderful place to get
smashed in?

you always think that, she says, you think
everyone is sitting around getting
smashed.

and look at *that* place, I say, it has windows
like a church. I bet they are sitting in there
smashed right now!

it isn't like that, she says.

I want to buy a place, I say, that I can get
smashed in. just a little place with the front porch
falling in . . . 2 hungry German shepherds . . . paint peeling
from the boards.

get it then, she says, get it.

it's somewhere, I say, I know it's somewhere.

we drive on into my court after stopping at the
liquor store. we have 4 bottles of white
German wine. we will get
smashed.

there's nothing like getting *smashed,*
especially under the right circumstances.
I mean, while you're not feeling *too*
bad.

they are always calling the police on
me around here.

I want to get *smashed* in a place like William Randy
Hearst's old castle.
I want to go from great room to great room
crashing full bottles against walls,
free within my own doom.

here among the poor there is no understanding
of the need for my sounds and my ways.
they must sleep their nights
to have strength for their factory days
so they are very quick to phone the law
even though it would seem to me
that they need to get *smashed* more than
anybody.

and when we get in she says,
well, are we going to have a quiet night?

and I say, I don't know.
I'm going to get *smashed*.

the image

he sits in the chair across from me,
"you look *healthy,*" he says in a voice that is
almost discouraged.

"3 bottles of white German wine each night,"
I tell him.

"are you going to let people know?" he
asks. he walks to the refrigerator and opens
the door: "all these vitamins . . ."

"thiamine-hcl," I say, "b-2, choline, b-6, folic
acid, zinc, e, b-12, niacin, calcium magnesium,
a-e complex, paba . . . and 3 bottles of white
German wine each night . . ."

"what's this stuff in the jars on the sink?" he
asks.

"herbs," I tell him, "goldenseal, sweet basil,
alfalfa mint, mu, lemongrass, rose hips, papaya,
gotu kola, clover, comfrey, fenugreek, sassafras
and chamomile . . . and I drink spring water, mineral
water and 3 bottles of German white wine . . ."

LOSE THE IMAGE

"oh," I said, "I am..."

"but how about your image?" he asked "people don't expect you to be like this..."

"disgusting isn't it?" I ask. "I've come down from size 44 to 38, I've lost 2I pounds..."

"I mean," he went on, "that you represented a man walking carelessy and bravely into death, foolishly, but with style,— Don Quixote, the windmills...."

"don't tell anybody, Ben," I answer, "and maybe we can save the image...?"

"you'll be going to God next," he said.

"my God," I answered, "is 3 good bottles of white German wine each night..."

"all right," he said, "I suppose it's all right."

"I still fuck," I said, "and I play the horses and I like to go to the boxing matches and I still love my daughter and I almost love my present girlfriend, maybe I even do..."

"all right," he said, "can you give me a ride back to my place?"

he looked a little bit sick.

"look, Ben," I said, "let me brew you up a little herb tea before we go? how about a touch of fengreek?"

"no," he said, "let's go..."

"all right," I said.

well, that's the way it was with friendships

they ended like affairs with women ended.

I locked the door and we went down the walk toward my car.

Charles Bukowski
11-17-77

"are you going to let people know?"
he asks.

"know what?" I ask. "I eat nothing that walks on
4 legs and I'm not a cannibal and kangaroos and
monkeys are out . . ."

"I mean," he says, "people thought you were a
tough guy . . ."

"oh," I say, "I *am* . . ."

"but how about your *image*?" he asks. "people don't *expect*
you to be like *this* . . ."

"I know," I say, "I've lost my beer-gut. I've come down
from size 44 to 38, I've lost 21 pounds . . ."

"I mean," he goes on, "that you represented a man walking
carelessly and bravely into death, foolishly but with
style like Don Quixote, the windmills . . ."

"don't tell anybody," I answer, "and maybe we can save the
image or at least prolong it . . ."

"you'll be going to God next," he says.

"my god," I say, "is 3 bottles of . . ."

"all right," he interrupts, "I suppose it's all right."

"I still fuck," I say, "and I play the horses and I like to go to the boxing matches and I still love my daughter and I almost love my present girlfriend, maybe I even do . . ."

"all right," he says, "can you give me a ride back to my car?"

"all right," I say, "I still drive cars."

I lock the door and we go down the walk toward my car.

[To Uncle Heinrich]
March 5, 1978

[. . .] I suppose I drink too much white wine but it is good stuff—Bereich Bernkastel Riesling—put out by Havemeyer—Produce of Germany—a white Moselle. I like to drink it while I'm writing and listening to symphony music on the radio. Linda has me on vitamins and herbs, fresh vegetables, no meats except fish and fowl, very little salt, sugar and sugar products, no beer or whiskey. I have come down from 223 pounds to 194. I should exercise more, but I don't want to make a *job* of anything. I am lazy except when it comes to writing—have written 330 poems in 3 months, wrote a novel in 5 months, a long one. There's nothing else to do, you know—play the horses, drink white wine and write, be true to Linda Lee and try to feel good, and I see my daughter down at Santa Monica now and then, she seems calm and thriving.

FROM

Women

One afternoon I was coming from the liquor store and had just reached Nicole's. I was carrying two 6-packs of bottled beer and a pint of whiskey. Lydia and I had recently had another fight and I had decided to stay the night with Nicole. I was walking along, already a bit intoxicated, when I heard someone run up behind me. I turned. It was Lydia. "Ha!" she said. "Ha!"

She grabbed the bag of liquor out of my hand and began pulling out the beer bottles. She smashed them on the pavement one by one. They made large explosions. Santa Monica Boulevard is very busy. The afternoon traffic was just beginning to build up. All this action was taking place just outside Nicole's door. Then Lydia reached the pint of whiskey. She held it up and screamed up at me, "Ha! You were going to drink this and then you were going to FUCK her!" She smashed the pint on the cement.

Nicole's door was open and Lydia ran up the stairway. Nicole was standing at the top of the stairs. Lydia began hitting Nicole with her large purse. It had long straps and she swung it as hard as she could.

"He's *my* man! He's *my* man! You stay away from my man!"

Then Lydia ran down past me, out the door and into the street.

"Good god," said Nicole, "who was that?"

"That was Lydia. Let me have a broom and a large paper bag."

I went down into the street and began sweeping up the broken glass and placing it in the brown paper bag. That bitch has gone too far this time, I thought. I'll go and buy more liquor. I'll stay the night with Nicole, maybe a couple of nights.

I was bent over picking up the glass when I heard a strange sound behind me. I looked around. It was Lydia in the Thing. She had it up on the sidewalk and was driving straight towards me at about 30 M.P.H. I leaped aside as the car went by, missing me by an inch. The car ran down to the end of the block, bumped down off the curb, continued up the street, then took a right at the next corner and was gone.

I went back to sweeping up the glass. I got it all swept up and put away. Then I reached down into the original paper bag and found one undamaged bottle of beer. It looked very good. I really needed it. I was about to unscrew the cap when someone grabbed it out of my hand. It was Lydia again. She ran up to Nicole's door with the bottle and hurled it at the glass. She hurled it with such velocity that it went straight through like a large bullet, not smashing the entire window but leaving just a round hole.

Lydia ran off and I walked up the stairway. Nicole was still standing there. "For god's sake, Chinaski, leave with her before she kills everybody!" I turned and walked back down the stairway. Lydia was sitting in her car at the curbing with the engine running. I opened the door and got in. She drove off. Neither of us spoke a word.

. . .

"Ladies and gentlemen, Henry Chinaski!"

I walked on. They jeered. I hadn't done anything yet. I took the mike. "Hello, this is Henry Chinaski . . . ."

The place trembled with sound. I didn't need to do anything. They would do it all. But you had to be careful. Drunk as they were they could immediately detect any false gesture, any false word. You could never underestimate an audience. They had paid to get in; they had paid for drinks; they intended to get *something* and if you didn't give it to them they'd run you right into the ocean.

There was a refrigerator on stage. I opened it. There must have been 40 bottles of beer in there. I reached in and got one, twisted the cap off, took a hit. I needed that drink.

Then a man down front hollered, "Hey, Chinaski, we're *paying* for drinks!"

It was a fat guy in the front row in a mailman's outfit.

I went into the refrigerator and took out a beer. I walked over and handed him the beer. Then I walked back, reached in, and got some more beers. I handed them to the people in the first row.

"Hey, how about *us*?" A voice from near the back.

I took a bottle and looped it through the air. I threw a few more back there. They were good. They caught them all. Then one slipped out of my hand and went high into the air. I heard it smash. I decided to quit. I could see a lawsuit: skull fracture.

There were 20 bottles left.

"Now, the rest of these are *mine*!"

"You gonna read all night?"

"I'm gonna drink all night . . . ."

Applause, jeers, belches . . . .

"YOU FUCKING HUNK OF SHIT!" some guy screamed.

"Thank you, Aunt Tilly," I answered.

I sat down, adjusted the mike, and started on the first poem. It became quiet. I was in the ring alone with the bull now. I felt some terror. But I had written the poems. I read them out. It was best to open up light, a poem of mockery. I finished it and the walls rocked. Four or five people were fighting during the applause. I was going to luck out. All I had to do was hang in there.

You couldn't underestimate them and you couldn't kiss their ass. There was a certain middle ground to be achieved.

I read more poems, drank the beer. I got drunker. The words were harder to read. I missed lines, dropped poems on the floor. Then I stopped and just sat there drinking.

"This is good," I told them, "you pay to watch me drink."

I made an effort and read them some more poems. Finally I read them a few dirty ones and wound it up.

"That's it," I said.

They yelled for more.

The boys at the slaughterhouse, the boys at Sears Roebuck, all the boys at all the warehouses where I worked as a kid and as a man never would have believed it.

• • •

That's the problem with drinking, I thought, as I poured myself a drink. If something bad happens you drink in an attempt to forget; if something good happens you drink in order to celebrate; and if nothing happens you drink to make something happen.

• • •

I took my bottle and went to my bedroom. I undressed down to my shorts and went to bed. Nothing was ever in tune. People just blindly grabbed at whatever there was: communism, health foods, zen, surfing, ballet, hypnotism, group encounters, orgies, biking, herbs, Catholicism, weight-lifting, travel, withdrawal, vegetarianism, India, painting, writing, sculpting, composing, conducting, backpacking, yoga, copulating, gambling, drinking, hanging around, frozen yogurt, Beethoven, Bach, Buddha, Christ, TM, H, carrot juice, suicide, handmade suits, jet travel, New York City, and then it all evaporated and fell apart. People had to find things to do while waiting to die. I guess it was nice to have a choice.

I took my choice. I raised the fifth of vodka and drank it straight. The Russians knew something.

• • •

My experience with Iris had been delightful and fulfilling, yet I wasn't in love with her nor she with me. It was easy to care and hard not to care. I cared. We sat in the Volks on the upper parking ramp. We had some time. I had the radio on. Brahms.

"Will I see you again?" I asked her.

"I don't think so."

"Do you want a drink in the bar?"

"You've made an alcoholic out of me, Hank. I'm so weak I can hardly walk."

"Was it just the booze?"

"No."

"Then let's get a drink."

"Drink, drink, drink! Is that *all* you can think of?"

"No, but it's a good way to get through spaces, like this one."

"Can't you face things straight?"

"I can but I'd rather not."

"That's escapism."

"Everything is: playing golf, sleeping, eating, walking, arguing, jogging, breathing, fucking . . . ."

"Fucking?"

"Look, we're talking like high school children. Let's get you on the plane."

It wasn't going well. I wanted to kiss her but I sensed her reserve. A wall. Iris wasn't feeling good, I guess, and I wasn't feeling good.

"All right," she said, "we'll check in and then go get a drink. Then I'll fly away forever: real smooth, real easy, no pain."

"All right!" I said.

And that was just the way it was.

fat head poem

I look up now and I am drunk in a roomful
of Germans. now the French are beginning to come
around,
and I've got to tell you
the French are hard drinkers too.
the Germans drink automatically
and they drink more than the French
but the French get more emotional:
they start to bitch about everything:
the old double-cross,
this bastard and that bastard,
they are more like American drinkers.

but I drank all the Americans out of
here long ago
and ran them out too.
the Germans and Frenchies are like space
creatures, they often speak in their own tongue
and this saves me from finding them
dull.
but I am getting tired of them
too.
the other day I ran off three
Germans. the French are next.

I await the Spaniards, the Japanese and the
Italians, then the Swedes...
~~my work has begun to appear in Spain and~~
~~Italy. all right. they can sit upon my~~
~~couch for a while,~~ also.

the Americans with their 6-packs of Coors
and their Marlboro cigarettes,
I don't need them anymore.
~~and I won't need them anymore~~
~~when I finally come out in paperback~~
~~from a large New York publisher~~
~~and my shit will be racked at Thrifty's~~
~~and at~~ L.A. International,
I ~~won't~~ need them.

all I'll need is for this Olympia
to keep charging down the stretch

picking up the front runners
one by one
charging past the Pulitzer prize
busting the wire
all the way past Moscow into
India...
east Hollywood was never a place for a
white tornado like
Chinaski.

THOROUGHBREDS

Charles Bukowski
6-29-78

I await the Spaniards, the Japanese, and the
Italians, then the Swedes . . .
the Americans with their 6-packs of Coors
and their Marlboro cigarettes,
I don't need them anymore.

all I'll need is for this Olympia
to keep charging down the stretch
picking off the front runners
one by one
charging past the Pulitzer Prize thoroughbreds
busting the wire
all the way past Moscow into
India . . .

east Hollywood was never a place for a
white tornado like
Chinaski.

FROM

Shakespeare Never Did This

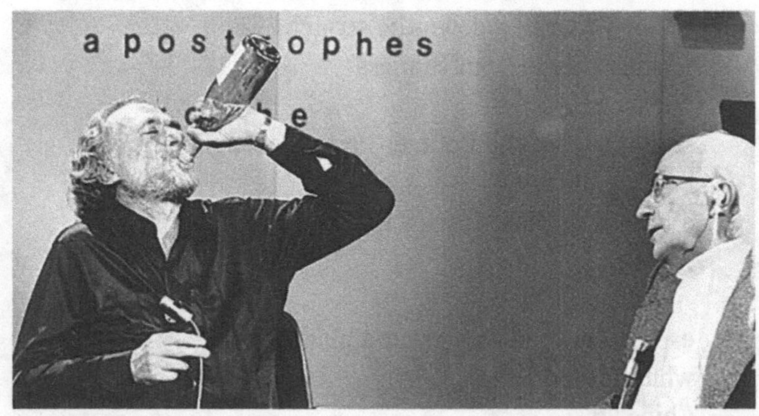

On Friday night I was to appear on a well-known show, nationally televised. It was a talk show that lasted 90 minutes and it was literary. I demanded to be furnished 2 bottles of good white wine while on the tube. Between 50 and 60 million Frenchmen watched the program.

I started drinking late in the afternoon. The next I knew Rodin, Linda Lee and I were walking through security. Then they sat me down before the make-up man. He applied various powders which were immediately defeated by the grease on my face and the holes. He sighed and waved me off. Then we were sitting in a group waiting for the show to begin. I uncorked a bottle and had a hit. Not bad. There were 3 or 4 writers and the moderator. Also the shrink who had given Artaud his shock treatments. The moderator was supposed to be famous all through France but he didn't look like much to me. I sat next to him and he tapped his foot. "What's the matter?" I asked him. "You nervous?" He didn't answer. I poured a glass of wine and put it in front of his face. "Here, take a drink of this . . . it'll settle your gizzard . . ." He waved me off with some disdain.

Then we were on. I had an attachment to my ear into which the French was translated into the English. And I was to be translated into the French. I was the honored guest so the moderator started with me. My first statement was: "I know a great many American writers who would like to be on this program now. It doesn't mean so much to me . . ." With that, the moderator quickly switched to another writer, an old time liberal who had been betrayed again and again but who had still kept the faith. I had no politics but I told the old boy that he had a good mug. He talked on and on. They always do.

Then a lady writer started talking. I was fairly into the wine and wasn't so sure what she wrote about but I think it was animals, the lady wrote animal stories. I told her that if she would show me more of her legs I might be able to tell if she were a good writer or not. She didn't do it. The shrink who had given the shock treatments to Artaud kept staring at me. Somebody else began talking. Some French writer with a handlebar mustache. He didn't say anything but he kept talking. The lights were getting brighter, a rather viscous yellow. I was getting hot under the lights. The next thing I remember I am in the streets of Paris and there is this startling and continuous roar and light everywhere. There are ten thousand motorcyclists in the streets. I demand to see some cancan girls but am taken back to the hotel upon the promise of more wine.

The next morning I am awakened by the ringing of the phone. It was the critic from *Le Monde*. "You were great, bastard," he said, "those others couldn't even masturbate . . ." "What did I do?" I asked. "You don't remember?" "No." "Well, let me tell you, there isn't one newspaper that wrote against you. It's about time French television saw something honest."

After the critic hung up I turned to Linda Lee. "What happened baby? What did I do?" "Well, you grabbed the lady's leg. Then you started drinking out of the bottle. You said some things. They were pretty good, especially at the beginning. Then the guy who ran the program wouldn't let you speak. He put his hand over your mouth and said, 'Shut up! Shut up!'"

"He did *that*?"

"Rodin was sitting next to me. He kept telling me, 'Make him keep quiet! Make him keep quiet!' He just doesn't know you. Anyhow, you finally ripped your translation earphone off, took a last hit of wine and walked off the program."

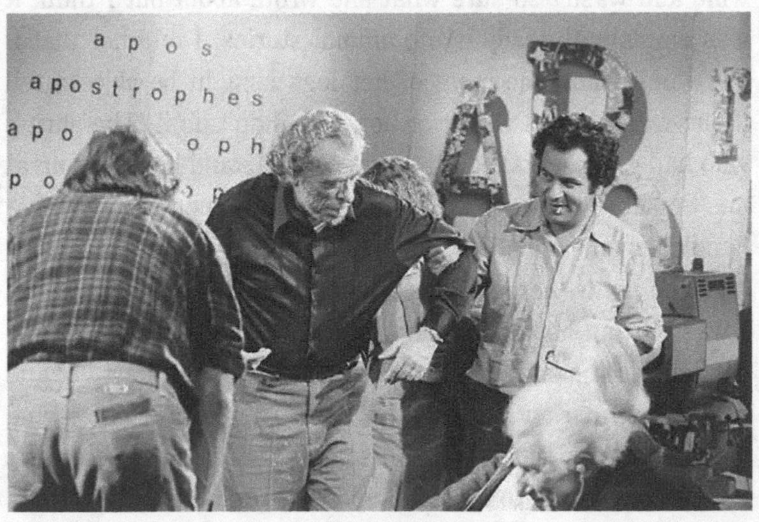

"Just a drunken slob."

"Then when you reached security you grabbed one of the guards by his collar. Then you pulled your knife and threatened all of them. They weren't quite sure whether you were kidding or not. But they finally got to you and threw you out."

• • •

The trip down [to Nice] took ten hours. We arrived at 11 P.M. that night. There was nobody to greet us. Linda made a phone call. Evidently they were in. I could see Linda talking and gesturing. It went on some time. Then she hung up and came out.

"They don't want to see us. Mother is crying and Uncle Bernard is raging in the background—'I won't have that type of man in my house! Never!' They watched the tv program. The moderator was one of Uncle Bernard's heroes. Uncle got on the phone and I asked him where they had been that day and he said they had deliberately gone out so they wouldn't have to answer the phone. He let us come all this way for nothing, he deliberately let us come all this way to get some fucking type of revenge. He told mother you were thrown off the station! It's not true, you walked off!"

"Come on," I said, "let's get a hotel room."

We found one across from the train station, got a second floor room, got out of there and found a sidewalk cafe that served fairly good red wine.

"He's brain-washed mother," said Linda, "I'm sure she won't sleep one bit tonight."

"I don't mind not seeing your uncle, Linda."

"It's mother I'm thinking of."

"Drink up."

"To think he deliberately let us take that long train ride for nothing."

"Reminds me of my father. He used to do little things like that continually."

Just then the waiter came up with a piece of paper.

"Your autograph, sir."

I signed my name and made a little drawing.

There was another drinking place next door. I looked to my right and there were 5 French waiters laughing and waving their arms. I laughed back, raised my drink to them. All 5 French waiters bowed. They stood a while at that distance, talking to each other. Then they walked off.

the drunk with the little legs

he fell down a stairway as a child
and they had to operate on his legs
and when they were done
his legs were about half the length
they were meant to be
and that's the way he grew into
manhood
with those very short legs
he hung around the Paris cafes
and sketched the dancing girls
and drank very much.
(it's strange that most of those
who create well seem to have some
malady.)
he was subsisting on his paintings
many of them used by the cafe
as advertising posters
when along came the beautiful
and terrible whore
and he painted her
and became involved
short legs and all.
she, of course, was hardly faithful,
and one night, defending her
faithlessness
she told him about his legs.

that ended the affair.
he turned on the gas jets
then shut them off
to finish a painting.

he was a little gentleman.
at least he was in this movie
I saw.
he liked to wear a top hat
and he sketched his things
while drinking;
doing it like that,
cutting through the odds,
he had it down tight and
clean,
he sketched all the dancing
girls
that would never be his,
and one night
he got it all down and
done,
tumbling drunk down a
stairway
little legs whirling
he became involved with that
other
terrible and beautiful
whore.

Hemingway

she said, it was in Havana in 1953
and I was visiting him
and one day I saw him
and it was in the afternoon
and he was drunk
he was stretched out on these pillows
drunk
and I took a photo of him
and he looked up and said,
"don't you dare give that photo
to anybody."

when she came from Italy this summer
to visit me
she told me about it,
and I said, "that must be some
photo."
she told me that my house was very
much like his house.
we drank, had dinner somewhere,
then she had to take a plane
out.

the photo is framed at the bottom
of my stairway now
looking north.

he was fat and he was drunk
and he's in the right
place.

Mozart wrote his first opera before the age of fourteen

I was all right when I moved in here: on the 3rd
day the neighbor to the east saw me
trimming the hedge and offered me his
electric hedge-trimmer.
I thanked him but told him I needed the exercise.
then I leaned down and petted his tiny quivering
dog.
then he told me that he was 83 years old
but still checked in at work every day.
it was his company and they did a million dollars
worth of business every day.
I couldn't match that so I didn't say anything.
then he told me that if I ever needed anything
to let him and/or his wife know.
I thanked him, then went back to the hedge.

each night I could see his wife watching television,
she looked at about the same things I did.
then one night I went mad on drink and ran up and
down the stairway screaming things at the woman I
live with. (some nights I drink 5 or 6 bottles of
wine and my mind becomes a freighter loaded with less
than evangelists; I usually scream loudly and dramat-
ically, running about naked; it lasts an hour or
two, then I go to bed and sleep.)

I did this type of thing twice during the second week
of living around here.
now I no longer see his wife watching television:
the venetian blinds are drawn closed,
and I no longer see the old man and his tiny
quivering dog
and I no longer see my neighbor to the west
(although on the 4th day I gave him many tangerines
from my tangerine tree.)

everybody has vanished.

come to think of it
my woman isn't even here tonight.

on the hustle

I suppose
one of the worst times was
when
after a drunken reading and
an all-night party
I promised to appear at
an eleven o'clock English
class
and there they sat
nicely dressed
terribly young
awfully comfortable.

I only wanted to sleep
and I kept the wastebasket
close
in case I
puked.

I think I was in the state of
Nebraska or Illinois or
Ohio.

no more of this,
I thought,
I'll go back to the factories
if they'll have me.

"why do you write?"
a young man asked.

"next question,"
I responded.

a sweet birdie with blue eyes
asked, "who are your 3
favorite contemporary
writers?"

I answered, "Henry Chinaski,
Henry Chinaski and Henry . . ."

somebody asked,
"what do you think about Norman
Mailer?"

I told them that I didn't think
about Norman Mailer and then I
asked, "doesn't anybody have a
beer?"

there was this silence, this
continuing silence and the class
and the prof looked at me and I
looked at them.

then the sweet birdie with
the blue eyes
asked,
"won't you read us
one of your poems?"

and then that's when I
got up and walked
out

I left them in there
with their prof
and I walked down
through the campus
looking at the
young girls
their hair
their legs
their eyes
their behinds . . .

they all look so good,
I thought, but
they're going to grow up
into nothing but
trouble . . .

suddenly I braced myself
against a tree and began
puking . . .

"look at that old
man," a sweet birdie with
brown eyes said to a sweet
birdie with pale green eyes,
"he's really
fucked-up . . ."

the truth, at
last.

night school

at the drinking driver improvement school
assigned there by Division 63
we are given yellow pencils
and take the test
to see if we have been listening
to the instructor.
like the minimum incarceration for a
2nd drunk driving conviction is:
    a) 48 days
    b) 6 months
    c) 90 days
there are 9 other questions.
after the instructor leaves the room
the students begin asking each other
questions:
"hey, how about question 5? that's a
hard one!"
"did he talk about that one?"
"I think it's 48 days."
"are you sure?"
"no, but that's what I'm putting
down."
one woman circles all 3 answers
on most questions
although we've been told to
select only one.

on our break I go down and
drink a can of beer
outside a liquor store.
I watch a black hooker
on her evening stroll.
a car pulls up.
she walks over and they
talk.
the door opens.
she gets in and
they drive off.

back in class
the students have gotten
to know each other.
they are a not-very-interesting
bunch of drunks and
x-drunks.
I visualize them sitting in
bars
and I remember why
I started drinking
alone.

the course begins again.
it is found that I am
the only one to have gotten
100 percent on the test.

I slouch back in my chair
with my dark shades on.
I am the class
intellectual.

fooling Marie

he met her at the quarter horse races, a strawberry
blonde with thin hips, yet well-bosomed; long legs,
pointed nose, flower mouth, dressed in a pink dress,
wearing white high-heeled shoes.
she began asking him various questions about the
horses while looking at him with her pale blue
eyes . . . as if he were a god.

he suggested the bar and they had a drink, then
watched the next race together.
he hit twenty win on a six-to-one shot and she
jumped up and down gleefully.
then she stopped jumping and whispered in his ear:
"you're magic, I want to fuck you!"
he grinned and said, "I'd like to, but when?
Marie . . . my wife . . . has me timed down to the
minute."
she laughed: "we'll go to a motel, you fool!"

so they cashed the ticket, went out to parking,
got into her car . . . "I'll drive you back when
we're finished," she smiled.

they found a motel about a mile and one half
west, she parked, they got out, went in, signed in
for room 302.
they had stopped for a bottle of Jack Daniel's
on the way and he took the glasses out of the
cellophane as she undressed, poured two.

she had a marvelous body and sat on the edge of
the bed sipping at the Jack Daniel's as he
undressed feeling awkward and fat and old
but also feeling lucky: his best day at the
track.
he too sat on the edge of the bed with his
Jack Daniel's and then she reached over
and grabbed him between the legs, got it, bent over
and kissed it.

he pulled her under the covers and they played.
finally, he mounted her and it was great, it was the
miracle of the universe but it ended, and when she
went to the bathroom he poured two more Jack Daniel's,
thinking, I'll shower real good, Marie will never
know.
I'll finish the day off at the track, just like
normal.

she came out and they sat in bed drinking the Jack
Daniel's and making small talk.
"I'm going to shower now," he told her, getting up.
"I'll be out soon."

"o.k., cutie," she told him.

he soaped up good in the shower washing all the perfume-
smell, the woman-smell, the sperm-smell away.

"hurry up, daddy!" he heard her say.

"I won't be long, baby!" he yelled from under the
shower.

he got out, toweled off good, then opened the bathroom
door and stepped out.

the motel room was empty.
she was gone.

on some impulse he ran to the closet, pulled the door
open: nothing but coat hangers.

then he noticed that his clothes were gone: his underwear,
his shirt, his pants with car keys and wallet, his
shoes, his stockings, everything.

on another impulse he looked under the bed:
nothing.

then he noticed the bottle of Jack Daniel's, half full,
on the dresser.
he walked over and poured a drink.
as he did he noticed a word scrawled on the dresser
mirror in pink lipstick: SUCKER!

he drank the drink, put the glass down and saw himself
in the mirror, very fat, very old.
he had no idea of what to do.

he carried the Jack Daniel's back to the bed, sat down,
lifted the bottle and sucked at it as the light from
the boulevard came in through the blinds.
he looked out and watched the cars, passing back and
forth.

[To Jack Stevenson]
March 1, 1982

[. . .] I did a lot of time in bars, mostly back east, mostly in Philly where the people were fairly natural and fairly inventive and fairly unpretentious. I don't mean they were any great wow, but even the fistfights were clean. I just got so I couldn't find too much on a barstool anymore, I gave it a long try. Finally, I just started taking the bottle or bottles up to my room and I found that I didn't mind that at all, I liked it, alone. Me and the drink, and the shades pulled down. Not thinking too much about anything. Just smoking and drinking, flipping through the newspaper, getting into bed and checking the cracks in the ceiling, maybe listening to the radio. When you realize that there isn't very much on the streets, somehow an old beat-up rug or say a chair with the paint peeling can have a certain native charm. Also, it's always nice to think about not being in jail or not trying to talk some ugly woman into your bed or trying to get rid of her the next day (when they start washing the dishes you know it's time to start putting on your crazy act). I guess with me it's really having more a taste for the drink than a taste for Humanity. Mix them together and you can waste a night easily, and that's not so bad unless the day has been exceptionally bad (like usual). Those Hollywood and Western bars, strictly dogshit havens—no heart, no line, no chance. I had a girlfriend who went to work in one of those places as a barmaid. Joint used to be called The Big Ten. I didn't say anything to her. I didn't complain. I just knew she knew less than I ever thought she did—I mean, no instincts, you know. I knew we were finished. I just let her drop into the bog and a new one knocked on my door, even worse. Well . . .

[To Gerald Locklin]
May 9, 1982

[. . .] Let an old man give you some advice. You know, man, that beer can kill you quicker than anything. You know what it does to the bladder, that amount of liquid just ain't supposed to pass on through the body, not even water. I know it makes for better conversation and keeps you out of alley fights behind the bar (most of the time) but the beer headache and the beer heaves are deathly. Of course, there's nothing like a good old beer shit. But a good wine will add ten years to your life as compared to drinking that green stuff out of the bargain pitchers. I know you prefer the bars and that when you ask for a glass of wine in a bar the tender reaches for this large dusty jug with a splash of dark coagulation hanging to the bottom, which is pure poison. I guess you just gotta go with the beer in the bars. The trouble with bars is that they're just like racetracks: the dullest and the most obnoxious go there. Well, hell, forget it. I'm drinking this here wine and rambling . . .

FROM

Ham on Rye

One day, just like in grammar school, like with David, a boy attached himself to me. He was small and thin and had almost no hair on top of his head. The guys called him Baldy. His real name was Eli LaCrosse. I liked his real name, but I didn't like him. He just glued himself to me. He was so pitiful that I couldn't tell him to get lost. He was like a mongrel dog, starved and kicked. Yet it didn't make me feel good going around with him. But since I knew that mongrel dog feeling, I let him hang around. He used a cuss word in almost every sentence, at least one cuss word, but it was all fake, he wasn't tough, he was scared. I wasn't scared but I was confused so maybe we were a good pair.

I walked him back to his place after school every day. He was living with his mother, his father and his grandfather. They had a little house across from a small park. I liked the area, it had great shade trees, and since some people had told me that I was ugly, I always preferred shade to the sun, darkness to light.

During our walks home Baldy had told me about his father. He had been a doctor, a successful surgeon, but he had lost his license because he was a drunk. One day I met Baldy's father. He was sitting in a chair under a tree, just sitting there.

"Dad," he said, "this is Henry."

"Hello, Henry."

It reminded me of when I had seen my grandfather for the first time, standing on the steps of his house. Only Baldy's father had black hair and a black beard, but his eyes were the same—brilliant and glowing, so strange. And here was Baldy, the son, and he didn't glow at all.

"Come on," Baldy said, "follow me."

We went down into a cellar, under the house. It was dark and damp and we stood a while until our eyes grew used to the gloom. Then I could see a number of barrels.

"These barrels are full of different kinds of wine," Baldy said. "Each barrel has a spigot. Want to try some?"

"No."

"Go ahead, just try a god-damned sip."

"What for?"

"You think you're a god-damned man or what?"

"I'm tough," I said.

"Then take a fucking sample."

Here was little Baldy, daring me. No problem. I walked up to a barrel, ducked my head down.

"Turn the god-damned spigot! Open your god-damned mouth!"

"Are there any spiders around here?"

"Go on! Go on, god damn it!"

I put my mouth under the spigot and opened it. A smelly liquid trickled out and into my mouth. I spit it out.

"Don't be chicken! Swallow it, what the shit!"

I opened the spigot and I opened my mouth. The smelly liquid entered and I swallowed it. I turned off the spigot and stood there. I thought I was going to puke.

"Now, you drink some," I said to Baldy.

"Sure," he said, "I ain't fucking afraid!"

He got down under a barrel and took a good swallow. A little punk like that wasn't going to outdo me. I got under another barrel, opened it and took a swallow. I stood up. I was beginning to feel good.

"Hey, Baldy," I said, "I like this stuff."

"Well, shit, try some more."

I tried some more. It was tasting better. I was feeling better.

"This stuff belongs to your father, Baldy. I shouldn't drink it all."

"He doesn't care. He's stopped drinking."

Never had I felt so good. It was better than masturbating.

I went from barrel to barrel. It was magic. Why hadn't someone told me? With this, life was great, a man was perfect, nothing could touch him.

I stood up straight and looked at Baldy.

"Where's your mother? I'm going to fuck your mother!"

"I'll kill you, you bastard, you stay away from my mother!"

"You know I can whip you, Baldy."

"Yes."

"All right, I'll leave your mother alone."

"Let's go then, Henry."

"One more drink . . ."

I went to a barrel and took a long one. Then we went up the cellar stairway. When we were out, Baldy's father was still sitting in his chair.

"You boys been in the wine cellar, eh?"

"Yes," said Baldy.

"Starting a little early, aren't you?"

We didn't answer. We walked over to the boulevard and Baldy and I went into a store which sold chewing gum. We bought several packs of it and stuck it into our mouths. He was worried about his mother finding out. I wasn't worried about anything. We sat on a park bench and chewed the gum and I thought, well, now I have found something, I have found something that is going to help me, for a long long time to come. The park grass looked greener, the park benches looked better and the flowers were trying harder. Maybe that stuff wasn't good for surgeons but anybody who wanted to be a surgeon, there was something wrong with them in the first place.

• • •

I raised my glass and drained it. "You're just hiding from reality," Becker said.

"Why not?"

"You'll never be a writer if you hide from reality."

"What are you talking about? That's what writers *do*!"

Becker stood up. "When you talk to me, don't raise your voice."

"What do you want to do, raise my dick?"

"You don't have a dick!"

I caught him unexpectedly with a right that landed behind his ear. The glass flew out of his hand and he staggered across the room. Becker was a powerful man, much stronger than I was. He hit the edge of the dresser, turned, and I landed another straight right to the side of his face. He staggered over near the window which was open and I was afraid to hit him then because he might fall into the street.

Becker gathered himself together and shook his head to clear it.

"All right now," I said, "let's have a little drink. Violence nauseates me."

"O.K.," said Becker.

He walked over and picked up his glass. The cheap wine I drank didn't have corks, the tops just unscrewed. I unscrewed a new bottle. Becker held out his glass and I poured him one. I poured myself one, set the bottle down. Becker emptied his. I emptied mine.

"No hard feelings," I said.

"Hell, no, buddy," said Becker, putting down his glass. Then he dug a right into my gut. I doubled over and as I did he pushed down on the back of my head and brought his knee up into my face. I dropped to my knees, blood running from my nose all over my shirt.

"Pour me a drink, buddy," I said, "let's think this thing over."

"Get up," said Becker, "that was just chapter one."

I got up and moved toward Becker. I blocked his jab, caught his right on my elbow, and punched a short straight right to his nose. Becker stepped back. We both had bloody noses.

I rushed him. We were both swinging blindly. I caught some good shots. He hit me with another good right to the belly. I doubled over but came up with an uppercut. It landed. It was a beautiful shot, a lucky shot. Becker lurched backwards and fell against the dresser. The back of his head hit the mirror. The mirror shattered. He was stunned. I had him. I grabbed him by the shirt front and hit him with a hard right behind his left ear. He dropped on the rug, and knelt there on all fours. I walked over and unsteadily poured myself a drink.

"Becker," I told him, "I kick ass around here about twice a week. You just showed up on the wrong day."

I emptied my glass. Becker got up. He stood a while looking at me. Then he came forward.

"Becker," I said, "listen . . ."

He started a right lead, pulled it back and slammed a left to my mouth. We started in again. There wasn't much defense. It was just punch, punch, punch. He pushed me over a chair and the chair flattened. I got up, caught him coming in. He stumbled backwards and I landed another right. He crashed backwards into the wall and the whole room shook. He bounced off and landed a right high on my forehead and I saw lights: green, yellow, red . . . Then he landed a left to the ribs and a right to the face. I swung and missed.

God damn, I thought, doesn't anybody hear all this noise? Why don't they come and stop it? Why don't they call the police?

Becker rushed me again. I missed a roundhouse right and then that was it for me . . .

barred from the Polo Lounge

once in Paris
drunk on national TV
before 50 million Frenchmen
I began babbling vulgar thoughts
and when the host put his hand over my
mouth
I leaped up from the round table of
various literary pricks
and tried to walk out
but the doors were locked
and manned by guards
but I was determined to get
the shit out of there
so I pulled my 6 inch blade
and demanded exit
as the guards backed off
regrouped
then charged me
grabbed my steel
and tossed me outside
upon my ass.

this time
it was about a recording
deal.
I was to meet various
producers at the
Polo Lounge
only they were late
so I found the bar and
began sucking it
up
until finally somebody
gave me a necktie
and I was led to a
table
where I was seated with
these producers and hangers-
on
and they ordered
dinner.
I passed, ordered
drinks.

I kept drinking.
then I had to piss
and I asked,
"where's the crapper?"
and they told me
and my girlfriend said,
"he gets lost so easy,
somebody ought to go
with him, he cracks up
when he gets lost."

but I told everybody
that I would be
all right

and I found the
crapper
pissed well

but coming out
I was lost at
once

and all my old
nightmares of being
lost
became reality

I wandered up and
down
among dozens of
tables
but mine had
vanished

and all the people
were contented and
superior

and I wandered about
and I got very
thirsty
so I walked over to
a table
lifted some guy's drink
and drank it down.

I thought it was very
funny
but the people stared
at me
with their paperclip
eyes
and so I started
talking to them
like what I thought they
looked like and felt like
to me
and then this guy
rushed up to me and he
was the
maître d'
and since he looked
over-startling
I pulled out my 6 inch
blade
pointed it a fingertip from
his stomach and said,
"now, *you* show me where I'm
sitting!"

and sure enough, he
did . . .

next morning I awakened,
popped up, asked my
girlfriend, "where are
we?"

she told me that we were
in a motel room.

"do you remember what
happened last night?"
she asked.

then I heard it: a
good friend of mine
had given the maître d'
$200 not to call
the police but
for the rest of my
life I was
forever barred from the
Polo Lounge.

"where the hell is our
car?" I asked.

"take it easy," she
said, "the car's out
back, I got up early
this morning and
checked."

"o.k.," I said, moving
toward the bathroom,
"now we can begin all
over again . . ."

trying to dry out

I am a drunk trying to stay off the bottle for
one night;
the tv has drugged me with stale faces that say
nothing;
I am naked and alone on the bed
among the twisted sheets I read the pages of a
supermarket scandal sheet
and am dulled with the treacherous boredom of
famous lives;
drop the paper to the floor,
scratch my balls . . .
good day at the track: made $468. I look
at the ceiling, ceilings are friendly like the
tops of large tombs;
I begin to try to remember the names of all the
women I have lived with . . .
soon enter a stage of half-sleep, the best kind:
totally relaxed yet semi-conscious under the over-
head light, the cat
asleep at my feet, the phone rings! I
sit up in terror, it's like an invasion and I
reach over
pick up the
phone

yes? . . .

what are you doing?

nothing . . .

are you alone?

with cat . . .

do you have a woman with
you?

just the
cat . . .

no . . .

that's good.

we say goodbye and I hang the phone up
then walk down the stairway into the kitchen
into the kitchen closet
get the bottle of 1978 Mirassou Monterey County
Gamay Beaujolais
and walk up the stairway, thinking, well, maybe
tomorrow night will be the
night.

speaking of drinking . . .

many curious things have happened to me while
intoxicated like awakening in some bed with a
woman I didn't know or in a jail cell or
injured or having been rolled
or any of the strange aftermaths of imbibing
or *during* imbibing like
one night while making what I thought was a
left against traffic into what I thought was
the driveway of a liquor store
only there wasn't any driveway where I thought
there was
and in that split-second of timing
I swung right to miss hitting the curb
and found myself driving straight into traffic
on a main and busy boulevard and
like in a mad dream
the first car to go past me
(in the opposite direction)
was a police car
and for some reason I
waved at the officer
then took a quick left at the next
corner and
zig-zagged through a series of
streets in order to
throw off his pursuit

and I eventually came upon
another liquor store
got my Jim Beam
and sneaked it up the back streets
to my place where I opened the
door
tripped on a throw rug near the
coffee table
and crashed against it
glass top and
all.

I awakened the next morning flat
against the coffee table
the 230 pounds of me having crushed all
four legs of the table under
but when I got up
the thin glass top was down there
unbroken . . .

I drank the Jim Beam that night to
celebrate my luck which
like anybody else's came more from
practice than
divinity.

FROM

Tough Company

Question: Your writing is permeated with drink. You're guiltless about it. There was a recent book by Donald Newlove, *Those Drinking Days,* which centered around the corrosive effect of drinking on American writers: Hemingway, Berryman, Mailer, etc. You have any brief pronouncements on the role of drinking in your life and writing?

Bukowski: There is a great sense of guilt attached to drinking. I don't share that guilt. If I wish to destroy my brain cells and my liver and various other parts, that's my business. Drink has gotten me into situations I never would have gotten into: beds, jails, fights, and long crazy nights. In all my years as a common laborer and bum, drink was the one thing that made me feel better. It got me out of the stale muck trap. The Greeks didn't call wine "the Blood of the Gods" for no reason at all. One hundred percent of my work was (is) written while drunk and drinking. It loosens the air, puts some gamble into the word. I don't think drink destroys writers. I think they are destroyed by self-satisfaction, the god damned ego. They lack durability because they've had to endure very little—some of them had just a bit, in the beginning. They start too fast, quit too early and are generally lower-level human beings. [. . .]

Question: Have your drinking habits changed since you've been a little more successful? You seem to have gone from beer and cheap wine to good wine and scotch. Are the drunks any different? Hangovers less painful?

Bukowski: I drink mostly good wine now, and drinking some, of course, right now. I now stay out of the bars, prefer to drink alone. And the better stuff makes for less fierce hangovers. Now I drink more hours but I drink much slower than I used to. All of which had increased the number of pages I type up. And I was always shamefully prolific.

40 years ago in that hotel room

off of Union Avenue, 3 A.M., Jane and I had been
drinking cheap wine since noon and I walked barefoot
across the rugs, picking up shards of broken glass
(in the daylight you could see them under the skin,
blue lumps working toward the heart) and I walked in
my torn shorts, ugly balls hanging out, my twisted and
torn undershirt spotted with cigarette holes of various
sizes. I stopped before Jane who sat in her drunken
chair.
then I screamed at her:
"I'M A GENIUS AND NOBODY KNOWS IT BUT
ME!"

she shook her head, sneered and slurred through her
lips:
"shit! you're a fucking
asshole!"

I stalked across the floor, this time picking up a
piece of glass much larger than usual, and I reached down
and plucked it out: a lovely large speared chunk dripping
with my blood, I flung it off into space, turned and glared
at Jane:

"you don't know anything, you
whore!"

"FUCK YOU!" she
screamed.

then the phone rang and I picked it up and
yelled: "I'M A GENIUS AND NOBODY KNOWS IT BUT
ME!"

it was the desk clerk: "Mr. Chinaski, I've warned you
again and again, you are keeping all our
guests awake . . ."

"GUESTS?" I laughed, "YOU MEAN THOSE FUCKING
WINOS?"

then Jane was there and she grabbed the phone and
yelled: "I'M A FUCKING GENIUS TOO AND I'M THE
ONLY WHORE WHO KNOWS IT!"

and she hung up.

then I walked over and put the
chain on the door.
then Jane and I pushed the sofa in
front of the door
turned out the lights
and sat up in bed
waiting for them,
we were well aware of the
location of the drunk
tank: North Avenue
21—such
a fancy sounding
address.

we each had a chair at the
side of the bed,
and each chair held ashtray,
cigarettes and
wine.

they came with much
sound:
"is this the right
door?"
"yeah," he said,
"413."

one of them beat with
the end of his night
stick:
"L.A. POLICE DEPARTMENT!
OPEN UP IN THERE!"

we did not
open up in there.

then they both beat with
their night sticks:
"OPEN UP! OPEN UP IN
THERE!"

now all the guests were
awake for sure.

"come on, open up," one of them
said more quietly, "we just want to
talk a bit, nothing more . . ."

"nothing more," said the other
one, "we might even have a little drink
with you . . ."

30–40 years ago
North Avenue 21 was a terrible place,
40 or 50 men slept on the same floor
and there was one toilet which nobody dared
excrete upon.

"we know that you're nice people,
we just
want to meet you . . ."
one of them said.

"yeah," the other one said.

then we heard them
whispering.
we didn't hear them walk
away.
we were not sure that they
were gone.

"holy shit," Jane asked,
"do you think they're
gone?"

"shhhh . . ."
I hissed.

we sat there in the dark
sipping at our
wine.
there was nothing to do
but watch two neon signs
through the window to the
east
one was near the library
and said
in red:
JESUS SAVES.
the other sign was more
interesting:
it was a large red bird
which flapped its wings
seven times
and then a sign lit up
below it
advertising
SIGNAL GASOLINE.

it was as good a life
as we could
afford.

my vanishing act

when I got sick of the bar
and I sometimes did
I had a place to go:
it was a tall field of grass
an abandoned
graveyard.
I didn't consider this to be a
morbid pastime.
it just seemed to be the best
place to be.
it offered a generous cure to
the vicious hangover.
through the grass I could see
the stones,
many were tilted
at strange angles
against gravity
as though they must
fall
but I never saw one
fall
although there were many of those
in the yard.

it was cool and dark
with a breeze
and I often slept
there.
I was never
bothered.

each time I returned to the bar
after an absence
it was always the same with
them:
"where the hell you
been? we thought you
died!"

I was their bar freak, they needed me
to make themselves feel
better.
just like, at times, I needed that
graveyard.

the master plan

starving in a Philadelphia winter
trying to be a writer
I wrote and wrote and drank and drank and
drank
and then stopped writing and concentrated on
the drinking.

it was another
art-form.

if you can't have any luck with one thing you
try another.

of course, I had been practicing on the
drinking-form
since the age of
15.

and there was much competition
in that field
also.

it was a world full of drunks and writers and
drunk writers.

and so
I became a starving drunk instead of a starving
writer.

the best thing was the instant
result.
and I soon became the biggest and
best drunk in the neighborhood and
maybe the whole
city.

it sure as hell beat sitting around waiting for
those rejection slips from *The New Yorker* and *The
Atlantic Monthly*.

of course, I never really considered quitting the
writing game, I just wanted to give it a
ten year rest
figuring if I got famous too early
I wouldn't have anything left for the stretch run
like I have now, thank
you,

with the drinking still thrown
in.

this

being drunk at the typer beats being with any woman
I've ever seen or known or heard about
like
Joan of Arc, Cleopatra, Garbo, Harlow, M.M. or
any of the thousands that come and go on that
celluloid screen
or the temporary girls I've seen so lovely
on park benches, on buses, at dances and parties, at
beauty contests, cafes, circuses, parades, department
stores, skeet shoots, balloon flies, auto races, rodeos,
bull fights, mud wrestling, roller derbies, pie bakes,
churches, volleyball games, boat races, county fairs,
rock concerts, jails, laundromats or wherever

being drunk at this typer beats being with any woman
I've ever seen or
known.

FROM

The Bukowski Tapes

I'm one of these types that always buys, I'm a sucker. Anyhow, so coming back, I'm carrying all these six-packs with three or four people, we're all laughing and all of a sudden this guy comes up.

He said, "Gee, you guys seem to be having a good time. You mind if I come along?"

They all said, "Yes, yes, yes!"

And I said, "Hey, wait . . ."

He said, "Oh, come on, let me come along."

I said, "All right, come on."

So we are all in, and we start drinking and drinking. There's a piano there. I go to play the piano. The night goes on. I can't play it, but I play it. And I'm sitting in a chair—I don't like this guy too much . . . He's talking about the war he's been in and how many people he killed. And that didn't interest me too much, you know, because in a war you can kill people and it doesn't mean anything. It's legal. It takes guts to kill somebody when it's not legal. Got it? So I told him this. He kept talking, bragging about various things: what a good shot he was, how many people he killed.

I said, "Bullshit, get out of here!"

He said, "You don't like me?"

I said, "Yeah, leave."

So he left a while, we're all talking and drinking. All of a sudden he came back. He had a gun. Suddenly I had no friends around me. They kind of disappeared away . . . and then he came up behind me, and he said: "You don't like me, do you?" This is the point where people often make a mistake. But I'm only going to talk about myself. I told him the truth.

I said, "No, I don't like you."

So he came up behind me and he put the gun to my temple.

He said, "You still don't like me, do you?"

I said, "No, I still don't like you."

Let me tell you something, I really wasn't frightened at all. It was almost like seeing a movie somewhere . . .

So he said, "Well, I'm going to kill you."

And I said, "Okay. Let me tell you something, if you kill me know you're gonna do me a favor."

It was true what I told him.

I said, "I'm a suicide case anyhow. I've been wondering how to do this thing, now you've solved my problem. If you kill me you've solved my problem and you've got a problem. You do life in jail or the electric chair, whatever the hell's going on around here."

There was silence. I could feel the gun just pressing on me. Just stayed there and I didn't say anymore, he didn't say anymore. Then he put the gun down and he walked toward the door, and the screen door slammed, he walked out . . .

So later, all my friends came around, "Oh, Hank, you all right?"

I said, "Yeah, you guys really helped me, didn't you? Just standing, watching. You couldn't have grabbed him from behind or anything."

"Well, Hank . . ."

I said, "Okay . . ."

So later it was discovered he'd gone into some drugstore with a gun and did something, smashed somebody with the gun butt, and tried to shoot and they put him in a madhouse, later. So, he was really for true, but you know there's nothing like one nut talking to another. I lucked it. But I was really ready to go. It wouldn't have been a big thing. And he knew it. If you don't feel the fear, you don't react.

• • •

*I think a man can keep on drinking for centuries, he'll never die; espe-*cially wine and beer . . . I like drunkards, because drunkards, they come out of it, and they're sick and they spring back, they spring back and forth . . . If you gotta be anything, be an alcoholic. If I hadn't been a drunkard, I probably would have committed suicide long ago. You know, working the factories, the eight hour job. The slums. The streets. You work a god damn lousy job. You come home at night, you're tired. What are you gonna do, go to a movie? Turn on your radio in a three dollar a week room? Or are you gonna rest up and wait for the job the next day, for $1.75 an hour? Hell, no! You're gonna get a bottle of whiskey and drink it. And go down to a bar and maybe get in a fist fight. And meet some bitch, something's going on. Then you go to work the next day, and do your simple little things, right? . . . Alcohol gives you the release of the dream without the deadness of drugs. You can come back down. You have your hangover to face. That's the tough part. You get over it, you do your job. You come back. You drink again. I'm all for alcohol. It's the thing.

. . .

We drank heavily and one morning I woke up with the worst hangover I ever had, like a steel band around my head. I really felt terrible and she was in the bathroom puking. We drank this very cheap wine, the cheapest you could get.

I'm sitting there almost dying. I'm sitting at the window trying to get some air. Just sitting there and, all of a sudden, a body comes down. A man fully dressed, he's got a necktie on, neatly knotted, he seems to be going in slow motion. You know, a body doesn't fall very fast. Evidently, he got up on the roof and just jumped off. This building is not very tall. I mean, he probably crippled himself for life. I don't know.

I saw him go by and I said, "Well, I don't think I'm going crazy. I think that was really a body that went by."

So, I hollered to the bathroom, I said, "Hey, Jane! Guess what?"

She said, "Ya, what is it?"

I said, "The strangest thing just happened."

"Yeah?"

"Yeah, a human body just dropped by my window. His head was on top and he was all lined up, and he was dropping through the air. He dropped right past the window."

She said, "Ah, bullshit."

I said, "No, no, it really happened. I'm not making it up."

She said, "Ahhh, come on, you're trying to be funny. You're not funny."

I said, "I know I'm not funny. Look, I'll tell ya what. Just come on out here, come to the window and stick your head out the window and look down."

She said, "All right, here I come."

She came, she stuck her head out the window and all I heard was, "Oh, God Almighty!"

She ran in the bathroom and puked and puked and puked. And I laid there, I sat there and I said, "I told you so, baby, I told you so."

And I went to the refrigerator, got a beer. I felt better. I don't know why I felt better. Maybe because I was right. So I opened my beer and I sat there and I drank it. I still didn't look out the window because I was feeling bad, and that's all there is.

[To A. D. Winans]
February 22, 1985

[. . .] On quitting your job at 50, I don't know what to say. I had to quit mine. My whole body was in pain, could no longer lift my arms. If somebody touched me, just that touch would send reams and shots of agony through me. I was finished. They had beat on my body and mind for decades. And I didn't have a dime. I had to drink it away to free my mind from what was occurring. I decided that I would be better off on skid row. I mean that. It had come to a faltering end. My last day on the job, some guy let a remark fall as I walked by: "That old guy has a lot of guts to quit a job at *his* age." I didn't feel I had an age. The years had just added up and shitted away.

Yeah, I had fear. I had fear I could never make it as a writer, moneywise. Rent, child support. Food didn't matter. I just drank and sat at the machine. Wrote my first novel (*Post Office*) in 19 nights. I drank beer and scotch and sat around in my shorts. I smoked cheap cigars and listened to the radio. I wrote dirty stories for the sex mags. It got the rent and also got the soft ones and the safe ones to say: He hates women. My income tax returns for those first years show ridiculously little money earned but somehow I was existing. The poetry readings came and I hated them but it was more $$$. It was a drunken wild fog of a time and I had some luck. And I wrote and wrote and wrote, I loved the banging of the typer. I was fighting for each day. And I lucked it with a good landlord and landlady. They thought I was crazy. I went down and drank with them every other night. They had a refrig. stacked with nothing but quart bottles of Eastside Beer. We drank out of the quarts, one after the other until 4 A.M., singing songs of the 20's and 30's. "You're crazy," my landlady kept saying, "you quit that good job in the post office." "And now you're going with that crazy woman. You know she's crazy, don't you?" the landlord would say.

Also, I got ten bucks a week for writing that column "Notes of a Dirty Old Man." And I mean, that ten bucks looked big sometimes.

I don't know, A. D., I don't quite know how I made it. The drinking always helped. It still does. And, frankly, I loved to write! THE SOUND OF THE TYPER. Sometimes I think it was only the sound of the typer that I wanted. And the drink there, beer with scotch, by the side of the machine. And finding cigar stubs, old ones, lighting them while drunk and burning my nose. It wasn't so much that I was TRYING to be a writer, it was more like doing something that felt good to do.

dark night poems

the faster you pour it down
the more immortal you
feel.

not immortal in the sense of
living forever
but immortal in the sense of
feeling you've almost lived
forever

and you're still here
in spite of
all
and
almost
in spite of
yourself.

• • •

why people want to get cured from
drinking is
beyond
me
although I realize there's a price
on the liver
the heart
and
everything
else

I am willing to pay that
price

people who fail at drinking
tend to fail
at many other things
also
and it's not the drink that's
the curse
it's the person
involved

this is a fine
second bottle

we look at each other
in the early
morning
and it is
a fine love
affair: direct
honest and
all-
consuming

and my fingers are still
upon these keys

as I think of Li Po
so
many centuries ago
drinking his wine
writing his poems
then
setting them
on fire
and sailing them
down the
river

as the emperors
wept.

FROM

"An Evening at Buk's Place"

Question: You used to do drinking contests, I think.

Bukowski: Yeah, I remember that. The drinking contests? Yeah, I often won them.

Question: Did you ever lose?

Bukowski: Not that many. But at the time I was very good. I could drink a lot, and I could outdrink about everybody. I think I've always had a taste for it, you know. It's pleasant. It feels good. And during these contests, all the drinks were free. It was very nice. And to get paid for drinking.

Question: Alcohol, wine, are they a kind of veil of illusion you throw upon reality? Or is it a way to see things more clearly?

Bukowski: Well, to me, it gets me out of the normal person that I am. Like I don't have to face this person day after day, year after year . . . The guy that brushes his teeth, he goes to the bathroom, he drives on the freeway, he stays sober forever. He only has one life, you see. Drinking is a form of suicide where you're allowed to return to life and begin all over the next day. It's like killing yourself, and then you're reborn. I guess I've lived about ten or fifteen thousand lives now. But a man who drinks, he can become this other person. He has a whole new life. He is different when he is drinking. I'm not saying that he is better or worse. But he is different. And this gives a man two lives. And that's usually in my other life, my drinking life, that I do my writing. So, since I've been lucky with the writing. I've decided drink is very good for me. Does that answer your question whatever?

Question: So you drink to write?

Bukowski: Yes, it helps my writing.

Question: Preferably wine, as you said.

Bukowski: Wine helps keep things normal. I used to drink beer and scotch together. And write. But you can only write for an hour, or maybe an hour and a half that way. Then, it's too much. But with wine, as I said, you can write three or four hours.

Question: And with beer?

Bukowski: Beer, well . . . you have to go to the bathroom every ten minutes. It breaks your concentration. So the wine is the best for creation. The blood of the gods. [. . .]

Question: In your young days, did you drink to prove your manhood?

Bukowski: Yeah, in the worst sense, yeah. We used to think that a man drank, you know. That drinking made a man. Of course, that's entirely untrue. And those ten years I spent just in the bars . . . An awful lot of people who drink aren't men at all, they are hardly anything. And they get on my ear, and they talked the most terrible dribble into my head you've ever heard . . . so drinking doesn't create anything. It's destructive to most people. Not to me, you understand, but to most people.

Question: To you it's not?

Bukowski: No, it's anti-destructive. [. . .] I do all my writing when I'm drunk. All the time I type I'm drunk. How can I complain? Should I complain about the royalties? I'm paid for drinking. They're paying me to drink. That's lovely.

immortal wino

Li Po, I keep thinking of you as I
empty these bottles of
wine.

you knew how to pass the days and
nights.

immortal wino,
what would you do with an electric
typewriter,
coming in after driving the
Hollywood Freeway?

what would you think while watching
cable tv?

what would you say about the atomic
stockpiles?

the Women's Liberation
Movement?

terrorists?

would you watch Monday night
football?

Li Po, our madhouses and jails are
overflowing
and the skies are hardly ever
blue
and the earth and the rivers
stink of our
lives.

and the latest:
we've begun to detect where God
hides and we're going to
flush Him out and
ask:
"WHY?"

well, Li Po, the wine is still
good, and in spite of it all, there is
still some
time
to
sit alone
and
think.

wish you were
here.

say,
my cat just walked in
and here
in this drunken room
this drunken night

are these
great yellow eyes
staring at
me

as I pour a
full glass of
this beautiful red wine

to
you.

cleansing the ranks

what I am talking about, he said, is the reformed alcoholic, they have
come by here, I have seen their flesh turn yellow and
their eyes drop out, their souls slack and
dull, then they start talking about how they never felt
better and that now life has true meaning, no more hangovers,
no more women leaving them, no more shame, no more guilt, it's
really great, it's really so great

but I can't wait for them to leave, they are horrible people,
even when they walk across the rugs their shoes leave no
marks, as if there is nobody there

then they mention God, quietly, you know, they don't want to
push you but . . .

I try not to drink in front of them, I don't want to force
them back into that evil
place.

finally, they leave . . .

and I go to the kitchen, pour a tall one, drain off half,
grin, go the other half.

none of the reformed I have ever met were grade-A
professional alcoholics, they just tinkered and
chippied with it . . .
I've been drunk for 5 decades, I've drunk more booze than
they've drunk water; what gets them in a silly tizzy
alcoholic shit-state is what I use to taper-off
with.

some people just fail at everything and what I am talking
about here is the reformed alcoholic: you can't be
reformed if you were never really
one.

one thing that makes it all so dull and
terrible: they all still claim to be alcoholics even after
they've stopped.

this is immensely resented by the true of the
tribe: we have earned our place here, feel worthy and
honored in our station, would prefer not to be
represented by worthless fakers: one can't give up
what one
never had.

FROM

"Gin-Soaked Boy"

Question: What was the period you drew on for the screenplay [*Barfly*]?

Bukowski: Actually, it was two periods and I melded them together. When I lived in Philadelphia, I was a barfly. I was about 25, 24, 26, it gets kinda mixed up.

I liked to fight—thought I was a tough guy. I drank and I fought. My means of existence . . . I don't know how I ever made it. The drinks were free, people bought me drinks. I was more or less the bar entertainer, the clown. It was just a place to go every day. I'd go in at five every day; it opened officially at seven, but the bartender let me in, and I'd have two hours free drinks. Whiskey. So I was ready when the door opened. Then he'd say, "Sorry, Hank. Seven o'clock. Can't give you any more drinks." I'd say that I'd do what I can. I was off to a good start, with two hours of whiskey. Then I'd get mostly beers. I'd run errands for sandwiches, get mostly beat up. I'd sit there till 2 A.M., go back to my room, then be back at 5 A.M. Two and a half hours of sleep. I guess when you're drunk you're kind of asleep anyway. You're resting up.

I'd go home and there'd be a bottle of wine there. I'd drink half of that and go to sleep. And I wasn't eating.

Question: You must have had a hell of a constitution.

Bukowski: I did have, yeah. I finally ended up in a hospital ten years later.

Question: Did you have a lot of energy?

Bukowski: No. Just the energy to lift a glass. I was hiding out. I didn't know what else to do. This bar back east was a lively bar. It wasn't a common bar. There were characters in there. There was a feeling. There was ugliness, there was dullness and stupidity. But there was also a certain gleeful high hitch you could feel there. Else I wouldn't have stayed.

I did about three years there; left, came back, did another three years. Then I came back to L.A. and worked Alvarado Street, the bars up and down there. Met the ladies—if you want to call them that.

This is kind of a mixture of two areas, L.A. and Philadelphia, melded together. Which may be cheating, but it's supposed to be fictional anyway, right? Must have been around 1946.

It seems that all the good old scum bars are disappearing. In those days, Alvarado Street was still white. And you could just duck inside and get 86'd in one bar and then move right down ten paces and there's another bar to walk into.

I've gone into bars with deadwood people and an absolute deadwood feeling. You have one drink and you want to get the hell out of there so fast. But this bar was a lively hole in the sky.

The first day I walked in, I got hooked. I just got into town. I walked out of my room—it was about two in the afternoon. I walked in and said, "Give me a bottle of beer." Picked it up and a bottle came flying through the air, right past my head. People just kept on talking! Guy next to me turned around and said, "Hey you sonofabitch, you do that again I'm gonna knock your goddamn head off." Then came another bottle flew past. "I told you, you sonofabitch." Then there's a big fiiiiight. Everybody went out in the back.

I said, "God, what a jolly, lovely place. I'm going to stay here." So I kept waiting for a repeat of that first lovely afternoon. I waited three years and it didn't happen. *I* had to make it happen. I took over.

I finally left. I said, "That first afternoon is never going to recur." I was sucked in. It was right after the war was over.

240 pounds

well, you get used to drinking, you have it
around all the time, and then in between the
hard drinking you rest up on beer and
wine.
then when you decide not to drink for a day
or a night,
here's a knock on the door and 2 or 3
people with something to
drink.

it's fattening.
I got up to 240 pounds and I'm only 5 feet
eleven and three quarter inches
but I blew out from under my neck,
a curving bow of flesh, no, bowl is more
like it, the too tight belt gripping,
cutting off the air, the belly hanging down
over the belt, the face overfull, the eyes
reddened, the skin
pitted and unhealthy.
another drink made you
forget.

the buttons ripped off my shirt front,
the sleeves were too short,
t-shirts were best, and blue jeans,
standing there bloated,
immense, puffing on a cheap
cigar, I didn't know
anything.

but I always drank until sunup
whether with somebody or
alone.

they no longer sold my pants
size in the regular stores
so I went to a big boy
store and the guy stopped me
at the door:
"you're not big enough!"
"all right, I'll see you in
a month."

I was too big for regular clothing
and too small for big boy
clothing.

also, the few women I knew said,
"god, don't get on top of
me!"

"o.k., baby, o.k., we'll work
something out . . ."

all that beer, wine, vodka, scotch,
whiskey, gin . . .
those morning bowel movements were
something . . .
the toilet bowel looked like somebody
had shoveled in 3 shovelfuls . . .
and the mess not only smelled like
excreta,
you still got the smell of whatever
was consumed the night
before . . . the scotch, the gin . . .
etc.

the problem was that the stench
lasted for 3 or 4 hours.
if a visitor happened by
they would say something like:
"what the fuck is that?
did somebody die in
here?"

I tried to solve that situation
by getting a fan and blowing air
about the bathroom
but that only spread the problem
all about the
courtyard.

I also puked a lot in the
mornings and found the best way
to settle the stomach was half a
glass of ale mixed with a half a
glass of tomato
juice.

one morning I was sitting at
the window facing the street
(I had the front yard) and
these two delicate boys walked
by.

"hey," I heard one of them say,
"that old guy in there is really
wild and weird, he's like a
Neanderthal man who has broken
his chain."

I really appreciated that:

recognized at
last.

FROM

Hollywood

[T]he screenplay began to move. I was writing about a young man who wanted to write and drink but most of his success was with the bottle. The young man had been me. While the time had not been an unhappy time, it had been mostly a time of void and waiting. As I typed along, the characters in a certain bar returned to me. I saw each face again, the bodies, heard the voices, the conversations. There was one particular bar that had a certain deathly charm. I focused on that, relived the barroom fights with the bartender. I had not been a good fighter. To begin with my hands were too small and I was underfed, grossly underfed. But I had a certain amount of guts and I took a punch very well. My main problem during a fight was that I couldn't truly get angry, even when it seemed my life was at stake. It was all playacting with me. It mattered and it didn't. Fighting the bartender was something to do and it pleased the patrons who were a clubby little group. I was the outsider. There is something to be said for drinking—all those fights would have killed me had I been sober but being drunk it was as if the body turned to rubber and the head to cement. Sprained wrists, puffed lips and battered kneecaps were about all I came up with the next day. Also, knots on the head from falling. How all this could become a screenplay, I didn't know.

I only knew that it was the only part of my life I hadn't written much about. I believe that I was sane at that time, as sane as anybody. And I knew that there was a whole civilization of lost souls that lived in and off bars, daily, nightly and forever, until they died. I had never read about this civilization so I decided to write about it, the way I remembered it. The good old typer clicked along.

• • •

Francine Bowers was back with her notebook.

"How did Jane die?"

"Well, I was with somebody else by that time. We had been split for 2 years and I came by to visit her just before Christmas. She was a maid at this hotel and very popular. Everybody in the hotel had given her a bottle of wine. And there in her room was this little wooden shelf that ran along the wall just below the ceiling and on this shelf there must have been 18 or 19 bottles.

"'If you drink all that liquor, and you will, it will kill you! Don't these people understand that?' I asked her.

"Jane just looked at me.

"'I'm going to take all of these fucking bottles out of here. These people are trying to murder you!'

"Again, she just looked at me. I stayed with her that night and drank 3 of the bottles myself, which brought it down to 15 or 16. In the morning when I left I told her, 'Please, don't drink all of them . . .' I came back a week and a half later. Her door was open. There was a large blood stain in the bed. There were no bottles in the room. I located her at the L.A. County Hospital. She was in an alcoholic coma. I sat with her for a long time, just looking at her, wetting her lips with water, brushing the hair out of her eyes. The nurses left us alone. Then, all at once, she opened her eyes and said, 'I knew it would be you.' Three hours later she was dead."

"She never had a real chance," said Francine Bowers.

"She didn't want one. She was the only person I've ever met who had the same contempt for the human race as I did."

Francine folded up her notebook.

"I'm sure all this is going to help me . . ."

Then she was gone.

2 Henry Miller paintings and etc.

drunkenness can have its advantages, like now, sitting alone in this room, one A.M. from the window I can see the lights of the city, well, some of them, and I look at them and become conscious of my hands, my feet, my back, my neck, and a small turning in the mind: being near 70 gives a long look back: the cities, the women, the jobs, the good times and the bad and it seems very *odd* to still be alive, puffing on a cigarette, then lifting this tall-stemmed wine glass while there is a wife downstairs who says she loves me, and there are 5 cats, and now my radio is blasting Bach.

drunkenness can have its advantages: I feel as if I have passed through 5,000 wars but now there are just these walls holding me together while there are 2 Henry Miller paintings downstairs.
I look back through my life and I do suppose that the most ridiculous thing I ever imagined was that I was a tough guy—I never could fight worth a fucking lick, I only thought I could and it cost me many times, but drunkenness can have its advantages: one A.M., confessionals toward the bartering hordes.

yet
who cares?
the final vote is not yet in.

I am tough.
tough enough to die well.

I look at the lights of the city, exhale a puff of blue smoke, lift my tall-stemmed wine glass, toast what is left of myself, of what is left of the world:
across continents of pain
I slice through like the last bluebird
winging it
dumbly.

the gigantic thirst

been on antibodies for almost 6 months, baby, to cure a case of
TB, man, leave it to an old guy to catch an old-fashioned
disease, catch it big as a basketball or like a boa-constrictor
with a gibbon, I'm put on the antibodies and told not to drink
or smoke for 6 months, and talk about breaking iron with your
teeth, I been drinking heavily and steadily with the best of
them and the worst of them and by myself for over 50 years, yeah.
and the most difficult part, pard, I know all these people who
drink and they just go on drinking right in front of me like
I'm not aching to crack their skulls and roll them on the floor
or on the ground or just the hell out of my sight—a sight which
notices *very much* anything microscopically alcoholic.
the second hardest part is being at the typewriter without it,
I mean, that's been my show, my dance, my entertainment, my
raison d'être, yep and how, mix booze with typer ribbon and you've
got a parlay where the luck rains night, day and in between, and
there's the phrase "cutting it cold" but I don't think that's
strong enough, it should be "chopping it cold" or "burying it
warm," anyhow it hasn't been easy, no no no no no no no no no no,
and I even had a dream where I was drinking somewhere and later
got picked up for drunk driving, and when I look at a bottle of
beer it looks like bottled sunlight, and a bottle of wine, espec-
ially the dark red, it looks like the life-blood of the world.

for drunks it is hard to think of a future: the immediate pre-
sent seems too overwhelming, so I forgive those who fail; these
almost 6 months have been the longest almost 6 months of my life.
forgive me for boring you with this . . . but what's that you're
drinking there?
looks good.
now, *you* talk and *I'll*
listen.

FROM

"Charles Bukowski"

Question: In one of your poems, you said you would drink heavily and then type all night. Your goal was to write ten pages before going to sleep, but you'd often write as many as twenty-three. Can you tell me about this?

Bukowski: I had just quit the post office and was attempting to be a professional writer at the age of fifty. Maybe I was scared. The chips were on the table. I was writing the novel *Post Office* and felt that my time was limited. At the post office, my starting time had been 6:18 P.M. So each night I sat down at 6:18 P.M. with my pint of Scotch, some cheap cigars and plenty of beers, radio on, of course. I typed each night away. The novel was finished in nineteen nights. I never remembered going to bed. But each morning, or near noon, I found all these pages spread across the couch. It was the good fight, at last. My whole body, my whole spirit, was wild with the battle.

Question: For you, is there a difference between writing done while drunk and writing done while sober? Does one state lend itself better to writing?

Bukowski: I used to always write while drinking and/or drunk. I never thought I could write without the bottle. But the last five or six months I have had an illness that has limited my drinking. So I sat down and wrote without the bottle, and it all came out just the same. So it doesn't matter. Or maybe I write like I'm drunk when I'm sober.

Question: Was Whitey a real-life friend of yours?

Bukowski: "Whitey" was an off and on drinking partner in this hotel on Vermont Avenue. I went there now and then to see a girlfriend and often stayed two or three days and nights. Everybody in the place drank. Mostly cheap wine. There was one gentleman, a "Mr. Adams," a very tall chap who took a fall down the long stairway two or three nights a week, usually around 1:30 A.M., when he was making a last attempt at a run of the liquor store around the corner. He would go tumbling down this long, long stairway, you could hear the sound of him banging along, and my girlfriend would say, "There goes Mr. Adams." All of us always waited to see if he would go through the glass doorway, which he sometimes did. I think he got the glass doorway about fifty percent of the time. The manager just had somebody come and replace the doorway the next day, and Mr. Adams went on with his life. He was never injured, not badly. The fall would have killed a sober man. But when you're drunk, you fall loose and soft like a cat, and there's no fear inside of you, you're either a bit bored or a bit laughing inside of yourself. Whitey just let it go one night, blood roaring from the mouth.

[To Carl Weissner]
November 8, 1989

[. . .] I fell off the wagon twice. My daughter got married and all those drunks about and all those free drinks about got to me. Free drinks, hell, *I* paid for the reception. Then about a week ago I gulped down four or five beers. Not bad for a lifelong alcoholic. Anyhow, the x-ray of chest came out clean—all white clouds. I'm free of TB and all related things. But will still take antibiotics until and thru Nov. 13, just to nail it down for sure.

Man, that was some shit. Months of being weak, coughing for 12 hours straight, no sleep, no appetite, almost too weak to walk to bathroom. Nothing to do but lay in that bed. I watched baseball games on TV I had no interest in. One good thing about TB, though, you don't have any visitors and that's great. I guess the best moment for me was when I managed to scrawl a couple of poems in a yellow notebook. [. . .]

Yes, I am going to begin drinking again but not as often. I like it, of course, when I'm writing and when there are visitors. People are more interesting to me when I am drinking.

Martin is bringing out another book in the Spring, *Septuagenarian Stew,* which is an admixture of poetry and short stories. One of the funny things is that many of the poems John selected were written during my recent illness period.

Which shows that I haven't slipped entirely. Makes one feel fairly good. I am still hooked on the typer, like to slip in the white sheets and bang bang bang bang at the keys. I am sick with writing. It is my drug. It is my woman, my wine, my god. My luck.

FROM

"Q&A"

Question: Does a relationship exist between the creative personality and the desire to use drugs or alcohol? If so, why?

Bukowski: Writers are mostly dissatisfied with life as life and with people as people, etc. Writing is an attempt to explain, escape and change the outrageous forces which make us more than unhappy. Drinking is a chemistry which also rearranges our horizons for us. It gives us two ways to live instead of one.

Question: Do you believe a large percentage of writers are alcoholics, or is that a myth?

Bukowski: I have known any number of writers and I am the only alcoholic I know. In fact, I am drinking as I answer these questions.

Question: Do you think some writers believe that while on alcohol or drugs they experience greater insight or a greater ability to see "truths"? Do they delude themselves?

Bukowski: Drinking oils the machinery but I doubt if it gives us any insights or truths. It just gets us going off our dead asses. It whirls the winds behind the gods. Besides, I drink when I don't write but, in a sense, I think I am writing then. The mind spreads to gather new surfaces, small imprints.

Question: Does living in a world dominated by technology require drugs as a door to perceive mythical levels of existence?

Bukowski: A drunk will use any excuse to drink: bad luck, good luck, boredom or maybe too much technology. Is drinking a disease? Is eating? So many things are needed to get us through. And if they aren't there, we invent them.

Question: Would you agree that addicted writers write well in spite of their addiction, as it has been said that Van Gogh was a genius in spite of his illness?

Bukowski: I think that the "illness" is in not being ill. I think that the most horrible people are the well-balanced, the healthy and the purposeful. Van Gogh is overrated but if he were around now I'd sure as hell hate to see him down working out at the corner gym.

Question: Can alcohol and drugs be surrogate friends for writers?

Bukowski: A writer has no friends, only distant allies. And I don't like to speak of alcohol and drugs in the same way. I fell into drugs for a while. I found that drugs made the mind indifferent to creation. Indifferent to everything. Alcohol made the muse dance; drugs made the muse vanish. For me.

Question: Have you ever written under the influence of drugs or alcohol? If so, how do specific drugs stimulate or retard your thought and visual processes? How do they affect your writing?

Bukowski: I drink when I write. It's good luck, it's background music. Wine and beer are excellent for long hours of good luck. Whiskey, hard drink, if you drink it the way I do, well, that's only good for maybe an hour. After that, you imagine you are creating the world's greatest masterpiece, only to awaken in the morning to pages of wasted dung.

Question: Is writing while experiencing the effects of drugs important to the creative process for you? Or are the benefits of drug use obtained at a time entirely separate from the act of writing?

Bukowski: Drinking is just fine, all by itself. In fact, sometimes it's a real savior, especially when you find yourself trapped with dull, lonely and unoriginal people.

Question: Truman Capote said that once he began writing, "in fearful earnest, my mind zoomed all night every night, and I don't think I really slept for several years. Not until I discovered that whisky could relax me." Have you used drugs or alcohol to escape the grip of obsessive writing, or to relax from the effects of creation?

Bukowski: When I read Capote I need a drink to get that thin crap out of my mind.

Question: If you do drink or use other drugs, is it at least partly to rid yourself of inhibitions and self-consciousness? Does it help to overcome the fear of exposing yourself? Do you think that there is a point of diminishing returns?

Bukowski: Only a jealous non-drinker would ask a question like that.

Question: Do you think drugs or alcohol can erode the creative process in the long run? Under what conditions can this be avoided, if it can be at all?

Bukowski: Drugs, especially, can erode the creative process. On drink, any gamble entails a possible loss but it's better to roll the dice than to sleep with the nuns. At the age of seventy, for the sake of my wife and my six cats and my daughter, I attempt not to drink every night. Still, my own death, I am ready for. It's only the other deaths that bother me.

Question: If you previously used drugs or alcohol and now abstain, how has that affected your writing?

Bukowski: That I wouldn't know.

hangovers

I've probably had about more of them
than any person alive
and they haven't killed me
yet
but some of those mornings felt
awfully near
death.

as you know, the worst drinking is done
on an empty stomach, while smoking
heavily and downing many different
types of
libations.

and the worst hangovers are when you
awaken in your car or in a strange room
or in an alley or in jail.

the worst hangovers are when you
awaken to realize that you have done
something absolutely vile, ignorant and
possibly dangerous the night before
but
you can't quite remember what it
was.

and you awaken in various states of
disorder—parts of your body
damaged, your money missing
and/or possibly and often your
car, if you had one.

you might place a telephone call to
a lady, if you were with one, most
often to have her slam the phone
down on you.
or, if she is next to you then,
to feel her bristling and outrageous
anger.

drunks are never forgiven.
but drunks will forgive themselves
because they need to drink
again.

it takes an ungodly durability to
be a drinking person for many
decades.

your drinking companions are
killed by it.
you yourself are in and out of
hospitals
where the warning often is:
"One more drink will kill
you."
but
you beat that
by taking more than one more
drink.

and as you near three quarters of
a century in age
you find that it takes more and more
booze to get you
drunk.

and the hangovers are worse,
the recovery stage is
longer.

and the most remarkably stupid
thing is
that you are not unpleased that
you have done it
all
and that you are still
doing it.

I am typing this now
under the yoke of one of my
worst hangovers
while downstairs now
sit various and sundry
bottles of
alcohol.

it's all been so beastly
lovely,
this mad river,
this gouging
plundering
madness
that I would wish upon
nobody
but myself,
amen.

the replacements

Jack London drinking his life away while
writing of strange and heroic men.
Eugene O'Neill drinking himself oblivious
while writing his dark and poetic
works.

now our moderns
lecture at universities
in tie and suit,
the little boys soberly studious,
the little girls with glazed eyes
looking
upward,
the lawns so green, the books so dull,
the life so dying of
thirst.

FROM

"Interview with Charles Bukowski"

Question: You seem to have a fascination with sex and alcoholism, what is this fascination?

Bukowski: Sex? Well I was drawn to it because I missed so much of it from basically the age of 13 to 34. I just didn't want to pay the price, do the tricks, work at it. Then I don't know, about at the age of 35 I decided I'd better get with it, and I do suppose that playing catch-up, I overdid it. I found it to be the easiest thing in the world. I found dozens of lonely women out there. I banged and slammed like a madman. I'd be one place or another. My car parked here or there. Dinners. Bedrooms. Bathrooms. One place in the morning, another place at night. Now and then I got caught. I'd meet one or another who'd make me feel real bad, they'd reel me in and hook me, work me over. Sharks. But as time went on, even I learned how to handle the sharks. And after a while, fucking and sucking and playing games lost its reality. I screwed so much that the skin of my dick was rubbing raw. Dry pussy? Sure, but mostly I knew the tricks, what to do, how to do, and then it got old and senseless. Sex is too often just proving something to yourself. After you prove it awhile there's no need to prove it any longer. But in a sense, I was lucky: I got all my fucking workouts before the advent of AIDS.

Alcohol is another matter. I've always needed it. It needs me. I've had any number of beers and a bottle of wine tonight within a couple of hours. Great. The singing of the blood. I don't think I could have endured any of the shitty jobs I had in so many cities in this country without knowing I could come back to my room and drink it off and smooth it out, let the walls slant in, the face of the subnormal foreman vanish, always knowing that they were buying my time, my body, me, for a few pennies while they prospered. Then too, I could have never lived with some of those women unless they were transferred by drink into half-dreams which wavered before me. Under drink, their legs always looked better, their conversations more than the lisping of idiots, their betrayals not a self-affront. Drugs I had no luck with. They took away my guts, my laughter. They dulled my mind. They limped my dick. They took everything from me. The writing. The small, tiny flick of hope. Booze rose me up to the sky, slammed me the next morning, but I could climb out of it, get going again. Drugs sacked me. Threw me on the mattress. A bug thing. If there is an out for the disposed, it's alcohol. Most can't handle it. But for me, it's one of the secrets of existence. You asked.

and it didn't even break

as a heavy drinker I often lost my
money or had it
stolen
so it got so when I became heavily
intoxicated I'd get to hiding my
money.
and I was very inventive.
the next day I never remembered
where I had hidden
it.
sometimes it took me hours to
find it.
sometimes days,
sometimes I never found it.

I won't belabor you with the many
strange places I hid my money
except for this one
time.
it was a goodly sum and it was
gone.
and after some days of searching
my apartment
I just gave up.

then one day I was shaving and I
noticed that my face seemed a bit
more out of contour than
usual.
I looked at the mirror and noticed
a bump pushing right out at the
center.
I got a screwdriver, undid the
screws and lifted the mirror
off.

the money fell to the floor.

drunk, I had unscrewed the
whole mirror, placed the
money behind it and screwed
it back on.

I felt pretty proud about that
one.
and more proud that I had
found it.

of course, that called for a
celebration.
I didn't even finish
shaving.
I went out and bought myself
a good fifth of
whiskey.

why not?
it felt like free
money.

tonight

so many of my brain cells eaten away by
alcohol
I sit here drinking now
all of my drinking partners dead,
I scratch my belly and dream of the
albatross.
I drink alone now.
I drink with myself and to myself.
I drink to my life and to my death.
my thirst is still not satisfied.
I light another cigarette, turn the
bottle slowly, admire
it.
a fine companion.
years like this.
but what else could I have done
and done so well?
I have drunk more than the first
one hundred men you will pass
on the street
or see in the madhouse.
I scratch my belly and dream of the
albatross.
I have joined the great drunks of
the centuries.
I have been selected.

I stop now, lift the bottle, swallow a
mighty mouthful.
impossible for me to think that
some have actually stopped to
become sober
citizens.
it saddens me.
they are dry, dull, safe.
I scratch my belly and dream of the
albatross.
this room is full with me and I am
full.
I drink this one to all of you.
and to me.
it is past midnight now and a lone
dog howls in the
night.
and I am as young as the fire that
burns
now.

[To John Martin]
October 20, 1992

Hello John:

Just two poems tonight but I think they do it.

Bush looks dried out of the game. And the billionaire guy talks a game he can't back. Clinton appears the best of the lot.

And so to bed. Sober tonight. I think I write as well sober as drunk. Took me a long time to find that out.

11/6/92 12:08 AM

I feel poisoned tonight, pissed-on, used, worn to the nub. It's not entirely old age but it might have something to do with it. I think that the crowd, that crowd, Humanity which has always been difficult for me, that crowd is finally winning. I think the big problem is that it's all a repeat performance for them. There's no freshness in them. Not even the tiniest miracle. They just grind on and over me. If, one day, I could just see ONE person doing or saying something unusual it would help me get on with it. But they are stale, grimy. There's no lift. Eyes, ears, legs, voices but . . . nothing. They congeal within themselves, kid themselves along, pretending to be alive.

It was better when I was young, I was still looking. I prowled the streets of night looking, looking . . . mixing, fighting, searching . . . I found nothing. But the total scene, the nothingness, hadn't quite taken hold. I never really found a friend. With women, there was hope with each new one but that was in the beginning. Even early on, I got it, I stopped looking for the Dream Girl; I just wanted one that wasn't a nightmare.

With people, all I found were the living who were now dead—in books, in classical music. But that helped, for a while. But there were only so many lively and magical books, then it stopped. Classical music was my stronghold. I heard most of it on the radio, still do. And I am ever surprised, even now, when I hear something strong and new and unheard before and it happens quite often. As I write this I am listening to something on the radio that I have never heard before. I feast on each note like a man starving for a new rush of blood and meaning and it's there. I am totally astonished by the mass of great music, centuries and centuries of it. It must be that many great souls once lived. I can't explain it but it is my great luck in life to have this, to sense this, to feed upon and celebrate it. I never write anything without the radio on to classical music, it has always been a part of my work, to hear this music as I write. Perhaps, some day, somebody will explain to me why so much of the energy of the Miracle is contained in classical music? I doubt that this will ever be told to me. I will only be left to wonder. Why, why, why aren't there more books with this power? What's wrong with the writers? Why are there so few good ones?

Rock music does not do it for me. I went to a rock concert, mainly for the sake of my wife, Linda. Sure, I'm a good guy, huh? Huh? Anyhow, the tickets were free, courtesy of the rock musician who reads my books. We were to be in a special section with the big shots. A director, former actor, made a trip to pick us up in his sport wagon. Another actor was with him. These are talented people, in their way, and not bad human beings. We drove to the director's place, there was his lady friend, we saw their baby and then off we all went in a limo. Drinks, talk. The concert was to be at Dodger Stadium. We arrived late. The rock group was on, blasting, enormous sound. 25,000 people. There was a vibrancy there but it was short-lived. It was fairly simplistic. I suppose the lyrics were all right if you could understand them. They were probably speaking of Causes, Decencies, Love found and lost, etc. People need that—anti-establishment, anti-parent, anti-something. But a successful millionaire group like that, no matter what they said, THEY WERE NOW ESTABLISHMENT.

Then, after a while, the leader said, "This concert is dedicated to Linda and Charles Bukowski!" 25,000 people cheered as if they knew who we were. It is to laugh.

The big shot movie stars milled about. I had met them before. I worried about that. I worried about directors and actors coming to our place. I disliked Hollywood, the movies seldom ever worked for me. What was I doing with these people? Was I being sucked in? 72 years of fighting the good fight, then to be sucked away?

The concert was almost over and we followed the director to the VIP bar. We were among the select. Wow! There were tables in there, a bar. And the famous. I made for the bar. Drinks were free. There was a huge black bartender. I ordered my drink and told him, "After I drink this one, we'll go out back and duke it out."

The bartender smiled.

"Bukowski!"

"You know me?"

"I used to read your "Notes of a Dirty Old Man" in the *L.A. Free Press* and *Open City*."

"Well, I'll be god-damned . . ."

We shook hands. The fight was off.

Linda and I talked to various people, about what I don't know. I kept going back to the bar again and again for my vodka 7's. The bartender poured me tall ones. I'd also loaded up in the limo on the way in. The night got easier for me, it was only a matter of drinking them down big, fast and often.

When the rock star came in I was fairly far gone but still there. He sat down and we talked but I don't know about what. Then came blackout time. Evidently we left. I only know what I heard later. The limo got us back but as I reached the steps of the house I fell and cracked my head on the bricks. We had just had the bricks put in. The right side of my head was bloody and I had hurt my right hand and my back.

I found most of this out in the morning when I rose to take a piss. There was the mirror. I looked like the old days after the barroom fights. Christ. I washed some of the blood away, fed our 9 cats and went back to bed. Linda wasn't feeling too well either. But she had seen her rock show.

I knew I wouldn't be able to write for 3 or 4 days and that it would be a couple of days before I got back to the racetrack.

It was back to classical music for me. I was honored and all that. It's great that the rock stars read my work but I've heard from men in jails and madhouses who do too. I can't help it who reads my work. Forget it.

It's good sitting here tonight in this little room on the second floor listening to the radio, the old body, the old mind mending. I belong here, like this. Like this. Like this.

wine pulse

this is poem #25 telling about how it's 2 A.M. and I'm still at the
machine drinking and listening to the radio and smoking this
cigar.
hell, I don't know, sometimes I feel like Van Gogh or Faulkner or
one of those—say Stravinsky; I just keep drinking the wine and
smoking, and there's nothing more magic or gentle than this, that's
why I tend to talk about it, I want to keep the luck going . . .
some critics say I write the same thing over and over.
well, sometimes I do, sometimes I don't, but when I do the
reason is that it feels so good, it's like I'm making love to
myself, but not really—it's to this machine, 2 A.M., the wine . . .
if you knew what I had here you would forgive me
because you and I know how temporary any graciousness is, and so
I play and brag and repeat:
it's 2 A.M.
and I am
Chopin
Celine
Chinaski
settling for everything:
one sweep of cigar smoke
another glass of wine
and the beautiful young girls
the criminals and the killers

the lonely mad
the factory workers,
this machine here,
the radio playing,
repeat
repeat
repeat
until what will happen to you
happens to me.

Sources

"ants crawl my drunken arms." *Literary Artpress* 2.2, Spring 1961; collected in *The Days Run Away Like Wild Horses Over the Hills,* 1969.

"What bothers me is when . . ." Excerpt from a March 25, 1961, letter to Jon and Louise Webb; collected in *On Writing,* 2015.

"Born Andernach, Germany . . ." Excerpt from a January 14, 1963, letter to William Corrington; collected in *Screams from the Balcony,* 1993.

"I just got to thinking . . ." Excerpt from an October 1963 letter to William Corrington; previously unpublished.

"I am getting a little drunk . . ." Excerpt from a March 1, 1964, letter to Jon and Louise Webb; collected in *Screams . . .*

"beerbottle." *The Wormwood Review* 14, August 1964; collected in *Burning in Water, Drowning in Flame,* 1974.

"brewed and filled by." (c. 1964); collected in *At Terror Street and Agony Way,* 1968.

"Confessions of a Man Insane Enough to Live with Beasts [#4]." (Early 1965); collected in *South of No North,* 1973.

"I wrote Henry Miller the other day . . ." Excerpt from an August 24, 1965, letter to Douglas Blazek; collected in *Screams . . .*

"I keep drinking beer and scotch . . ." Excerpt from a 1965 letter to William Wantling; collected in *Screams . . .*

"Buffalo Bill." *The Wormwood Review* 24, March 1966; collected in *The Roominghouse Madrigals*, 1988.

"Notes of a Dirty Old Man." *Open City* 23, October 4, 1967; collected in *Notes of a Dirty Old Man*, 1969.

"The Great Zen Wedding." (September 1969); collected in *Erections, Ejaculations, Exhibitions, and General Tales of Ordinary Madness*, 1972.

"In bed I had something . . ." (February 1970); excerpt from *Post Office*, 1971.

"short non-moon shots to nowhere [#16]." *Jeopardy* 6, March 1970; collected as "millionaires" in *Mockingbird Wish Me Luck*, 1972.

"nobody understands an alcoholic . . ." Excerpt from a December 1, 1970, letter to Lafayette Young; collected in *Living on Luck*, 1995.

"drinking's good for a guy your age . . ." Excerpt from a March 1, 1971, letter to Steve Richmond; previously unpublished.

"I'm on the wagon . . ." Excerpt from a March 22, 1971, letter to John Bennett; previously unpublished.

"on the wagon." March 31, 1971, manuscript; previously uncollected.

"drinking." April 6, 1971, manuscript; previously uncollected.

"the angels of Sunday." *Mano-Mano* 2, July 1971; previously uncollected.

"Charles Bukowski Answers 10 Easy Questions," *Throb* 2, Summer–Fall 1971.

"drunk ol' Bukowski drunk." 1971 manuscript; collected in *Mockingbird* . . .

"Notes on the Life of an Aged Poet," January 24, 1972, manuscript; collected in *Portions from a Wine-Stained Notebook*, 2009.

"my landlady and my landlord." Early 1972 manuscript; collected in *Mockingbird*...

"The Blinds." 1972 manuscript; later reworked and incorporated into *Factotum,* 1975.

"Notes of a Dirty Old Man." *Los Angeles Free Press* 428, October 2, 1972; collected as "This Is What Killed Dylan Thomas" in *South of No North*.

"another poem about a drunk and then I'll let you go." *Los Angeles Free Press* 456, April 13, 1973; collected in *The People Look Like Flowers at Last*, 2007. A longer version of this poem, titled "wax job," was previously collected in *Burning* . . .

"in the name of love and art." *Second Coming* 2.1/2, Summer 1973; previously uncollected.

"the drunk tank judge." June 14, 1973, manuscript; collected in *Play the Piano Like a Percussion Instrument Until the Fingers Begin to Bleed a Bit,* 1979.

"some people never go crazy." *Two Charlies* 3, 1973; collected as "some people" in *Burning* . . .

"Notes of a Dirty Old Man." *Los Angeles Free Press* 465, June 15, 1973; collected in *More Notes of a Dirty Old Man*, 2011.

"Confessions of a Badass Poet," *Berkeley Barb* 454, April 26, 1974.

"some picnic." *Wormwood Review* 55, 1974; collected in *Love Is a Dog from Hell,* 1977.

"18,000 to one." November 25, 1974 manuscript (second draft); collected as "38,000 to one" in *What Matters Most Is How Well You Walk Through the Fire,* 1999.

"Paying for Horses: An Interview with Charles Bukowski," *London Magazine* 14.5, December 1974/January 1975.

"I awakened much later . . ." Excerpts from *Factotum*, 1975. The first excerpt is based on a June 30, 1972, "Notes of a Dirty Old Man" column published in the *Los Angeles Free Press*.

"ah, shit." January 25, 1976, manuscript; collected as "ah . . ." in *Love Is a Dog* . . .

"who in the hell is Tom Jones?" June 4, 1975, manuscript; collected in *Love Is a Dog* . . .

"beer." June 5, 1976, manuscript; collected in *Love Is a Dog* . . .

"shit time." *Love Is a Dog* . . .

"Buk: The Pock-Marked Poetry of Charles Bukowski. Notes of a Dirty Old Mankind," *Rolling Stone* 215, June 17, 1976.

"Charles Bukowski. Dialog with a Dirty Old Man," *Hustler* 3.6, December 1976.

"smashed." November 2, 1977, manuscript; previously uncollected.

"the image." November 17, 1977, manuscript (second draft); collected in *What Matters Most* . . .

"I suppose I drink too much white wine . . ." Excerpt from a March 5, 1978, letter to Uncle Heinrich; previously unpublished.

"One afternoon I was coming from the liquor store . . ." Excerpts from *Women*, 1978.

"fat head poem." June 29, 1978, manuscript; collected in *Shakespeare Never Did This*, 1995.

"On Friday night I was to appear . . ." Excerpts from *Shakespeare* . . .

"the drunk with the little legs." September 26, 1979, manuscript; collected as "Toulouse" in *Open All Night*.

"Hemingway." June 28, 1979, manuscript (first draft); previously uncollected. A very similar poem, titled

"Hemingway, drunk before noon," written in 1985, was collected as "drunk before noon" in *The Night Torn Mad With Footsteps,* 2001.

"Mozart wrote his first opera before the age of fourteen." *Harbor Review,* Spring 1980; collected as "night sweats" in *Open All Night.*

"on the hustle." March 10, 1980, manuscript; collected in *Dangling in Tournefortia,* 1981.

"night school." *The Wormwood Review* 81/82, 1981; collected in *Dangling . . .*

"fooling Marie." January 17, 1982, manuscripts; collected as "fooling Marie (the poem)" in *Come On In,* 2006.

"I did a lot of time in bars . . ." Excerpt from a March 1, 1982, letter to Jack Stevenson; previously unpublished.

"Let an old man give you some advice . . ." Excerpt from a May 9, 1982, letter to Gerald Locklin; collected in *Reach for the Sun,* 1999.

"One day, just like in grammar school . . ." Excerpts from *Ham on Rye,* 1982.

"barred from the Polo Lounge." May 1983 manuscript; previously uncollected.

"trying to dry out." June 22, 1983, manuscript (second draft); collected in *The Continual Condition,* 2009.

"speaking of drinking . . ." August 20, 1983, manuscript; previously uncollected.

Tough Company, by Tom Russell, February 2008. These interview excerpts were first published in January 1984 in the Norwegian magazine *Puls.*

"40 years ago in that hotel room." February 1984 manuscript; collected in *The Night Torn . . .*

"my vanishing act." October 1984 manuscript; collected in *You Get So Alone at Times That It Just Makes Sense,* 1986.

"the master plan." November 1984 manuscript; collected in *You Get So Alone . . .*

"this." December 1984 manuscript; collected in *You Get So Alone . . .*

The Charles Bukowski Tapes, directed by Barbet Schroeder, January 1985.

"On quitting your job at 50 . . ." Excerpt from a February 22, 1985, letter to A. D. Winans; collected in *On Writing.*

"dark night poems [#6 and #11]." November 1985 manuscript; previously uncollected.

"An Evening at Buk's Place." This interview, conducted on February 17, 1986, was later collected in Jean-François Duval's *Bukowski and the Beats. A Commentary on the Beat Generation,* 2002.

"immortal wino." October 16, 1986, manuscript; collected in *Septuagenarian Stew,* 1990.

"cleansing the ranks." *Water Row Review* 1, 1987; collected in *Septuagenarian . . .*

"Gin-Soaked Boy," *Film Comment* 23.4, July/August 1987.

"240 pounds." 1988 manuscript; previously uncollected.

"The screenplay began to move . . ." Excerpts from *Hollywood,* 1989.

"2 Henry Miller paintings and etc." 1989 manuscript; previously uncollected.

"the gigantic thirst." Late 1989 manuscript; collected in *The People Look Like . . .*

"Charles Bukowski," *Arete* 2.1, July–August 1989.

"I fell off the wagon twice . . ." Excerpt from a November 8, 1989, letter to Carl Weissner; previously unpublished.

"Q&A," *Arete* 2.6, Summer 1990.

"hangovers." (Early 1991); *The Last Night of the Earth Poems,* 1992.

"the replacements." c. 1991 manuscript; collected in *The Last Night . . .*

"Interview with Charles Bukowski," *Lizard's Eyelid*, c. 1992.

"and it didn't even break." June 11, 1992, manuscript; previously uncollected.

"tonight." June 1992 manuscript; collected as "a fine madness" in *The Continual . . .*

"Hello John: Just two poems tonight . . ." October 20, 1992, letter to John Martin; previously unpublished.

"11/6/92 12:08 AM." *Spillway. New Directions in Poetry* 5, 1996; collected in *The Captain Is Out to Lunch and the Sailors Have Taken Over the Ship*, 1998.

"wine pulse." February 29, 1984, manuscript; collected in *The Night Torn Mad . . .*

Acknowledgments

The editor and publisher would like to thank the owners of the poems here printed, which include the following institutions:

University of Arizona, Special Collections
The University of California, Los Angeles,
Special Collections
The University of California, Santa Barbara,
Special Collections
The Huntington Library, San Marino, California
Indiana University, Lilly Library
The University of Southern California,
Rare Books Collection

Thanks also to the following publishers and periodicals, where some of the poems, short stories, and interviews were first printed: *Arete, Literary Artpress, Berkeley Barb,* City Lights, *Film Comment, Hustler, Jeopardy, Lizard's Eyelid, London Magazine, Los Angeles Free Press, Mano-Mano,* Mystery Island Publications, *Rolling Stone, Second Coming, Spillway,* Sun Dog Press, *Throb, Two Charlies, Water Row Review,* and *Wormwood Review*.

To Ona and Gara, for saying go when all else says stop.

To Linda Bukowski, for such passion in keeping the flame alive—keep on trucking!

To Bukowski, for exploring uncharted territory against all odds, drink in hand.

Printed in the USA
CPSIA information can be obtained
at www.ICGtesting.com
JSHW031058180424
61399JS00013B/415

9 780062 857941